Giving students effective written feedback

Giving students effective written feedback

Deirdre Burke and Jackie Pieterick

 Open University Press

Open University Press
McGraw-Hill Education
McGraw-Hill House
Shoppenhangers Road
Maidenhead
Berkshire
England
SL6 2QL

email: enquiries@openup.co.uk
world wide web: www.openup.co.uk

and Two Penn Plaza, New York, NY 10121-2289, USA

First published 2010

A catalogue record of this book is available from the British Library

ISBN-13: 978-0-33-523745-6 (pb)   978-0-33-523744-9 (hb)
ISBN-10: 0335237452 (pb)   0335237444 (hb)

Library of Congress Cataloguing-in-Publication Data
CIP data applied for

Typeset by RefineCatch Limited, Bungay, Suffolk
Printed in the UK by Bell & Bain Ltd, Glasgow

Fictitious names of companies, products, people, characters and/or
data that may be used herein (in case studies or in examples) are not
intended to represent any real individual, company, product or event.

Mixed Sources
Product group from well-managed
forests and other controlled sources
www.fsc.org Cert no. TT-COC-002769
© 1996 Forest Stewardship Council

The *McGraw·Hill* Companies

Contents

List of tables and figures

Tables

Figure

List of boxes

List of activities

Introduction

Why this book? • *What is feedback?* • *Our approach* • *Practical approaches*
• *A timely publication* • *Activities and case studies*

Why this book?

Askew and Lodge noted that 'feedback is a rather small notion to write a whole book about' (2000: 1) but justified their approach as 'it is time that understandings about feedback in education are examined more closely'. We note that tutor written feedback is an even smaller 'notion to write a book about', but justify our approach on the need to examine the particular issues surrounding written feedback more closely.

Why, we have been asked, do you want to focus a book on written feedback? Surely there is a vast amount of literature already available on the topic of tutor feedback? Also why do you want to differentiate written feedback from other types of feedback; wouldn't it have made sense to deal with all types of feedback? These questions may have occurred to you as you picked up the book, so we will explain why we feel our approach is justified.

First, there is a vast literature on assessment that includes sections on feedback. There are also a number of texts that focus specifically on tutor feedback. But we have been unable to find the text that we as tutors were looking for, one that helped us to develop our understanding, as tutors, of the impact our written feedback might have on students. We wanted a text that helped us to develop our practice so that students used our feedback to improve their learning. Finally, we sought a text that brought together the issues concerning the provision of feedback by tutors and the reception of feedback by students.

Second, from our individual perspectives as a writing tutor and a subject tutor, we felt that the issues we needed to explore, in a reasonably short text, were specific to the medium of written (or typed) feedback. Thus, this single focus would enable us to explore both sides of this feedback communication: the practice of tutors in the provision of written feedback, and the guidance provided to students for the reception and use of feedback.

Like Murray and Moore's *Handbook of Academic Writing*, our text aims to help tutors develop a conceptual understanding of feedback issues at their own level, before moving on to consider specific strategies that can be used to make feedback more effective. In particular we share the same concern to recognize the impact of 'disciplinarity' in tutor practice, with the case studies providing practical insights into the practice of specific disciplines.

Thus, our focus is on tutor written feedback on student written work. Our aim is to draw on relevant research in the field to develop understanding of underlying principles and issues. We offer short annotations to bibliographical entries to help you decide which texts are worth following up. Our own research and practice are drawn on to contextualize issues and explore possible developments to improve the effectiveness of feedback. This 'effectiveness' addresses both the time and energy put into the provision of feedback by tutors, and the intellectual and emotional engagement with this feedback by students.

However, the issues of written feedback are complex and there is no simple strategy to meet the needs of all involved in higher education. It is not possible to provide a 'one fit for all' strategy; rather we aim to present a range of issues and practical applications that can be drawn on to meet the needs of particular situations.

Giving Students Effective Written Feedback recognizes tutors' written feedback to be an area that requires specific and detailed consideration in order to share related research and to explore practical strategies to improve the provision and use of tutor feedback. An additional feature of this text is the recognition of the important role that institutional staff, from a range of areas, make to student learning. The final chapter on 'Feedback and personal development planning', for example, explores the range of potential avenues of support for students in the unpacking of and acting on tutor feedback. This exploration may bring new awareness to subject tutors on the range of staff available to help support and develop student learning, and thus feed into subject policies for student support. Similarly, those in student support may find the tutor-focused sections help contextualize the queries students raise about the tutor feedback on their work. This bringing together of all staff involved in the support of student learning is an important feature of this text; we need to be aware of each other's roles so that we can identify the appropriate support for student learners.

What is feedback?

A good starting point is the etymology of the term feedback, so that we can be working from a clear understanding of the term. It's important that we conceive the task providing feedback as being more than marking or assessing.

Activity: Defining feedback

How would you define feedback?
Now consider the following and whether they offer anything to your own definition.

1 Thorndike's Law of Effect: feedback as 'knowledge of the results and reinforcement of the right answer' (McKeachie 1974: 7).
2 Feedback is 'the process of returning part of the output of a circuit, system, or device to the input, either to oppose the input (negative feedback) or to aid the input (positive feedback)' (dictionary.com).
3 Benne defined feedback as 'verbal and nonverbal responses from others to a unit of behaviour provided as close in time to the behaviour as possible, and capable of being perceived and utilised by the individual initiating the behaviour' (in Knight 1995: 158).
4 'Feedback started in the early twentieth century, with the advent of microphones. Since inputs into the mics were "feeds", and they were designed to only work with inputs, if there were "feeds" that came back through the system [usually from being too close to speakers], you'd get an awful noise. That awful noise was named "feedback", because it was a "feed" that came "back" into the system' (Man 2008).

Feedback as 'that awful noise': this last definition raises an interesting perspective. This negative view of feedback as an unwanted consequence of the input has direct relevance for our approach. Often tutor feedback is perceived by students negatively, and we are sure some students would accept the description of feedback as 'awful noise'. Tutor feedback can have a negative impact on students; it can crush their confidence, destroy their motivation and render them impotent for future learning. We need to be aware that our feedback could be seen as opposing the input, i.e. student learning, and have the long-term consequence of limiting future learning.

Giving Students Effective Written Feedback therefore intends to help redirect tutors' and students' use of feedback by moving it closer to Kurt Lewin's (1948) definition. Lewin, the father of action research, revised ways of thinking about feedback in the 1940s by adopting the term from electrical engineering and rocket science. Rockets are designed so their courses can be corrected or altered at any time during the flight to the target through a series of signals exchanged between the rocket and its earth station. In this sense, then, feedback is a positive, reciprocal arrangement in which tutors' written comments signal information to students about how well they are on course to their target, and students in turn use the comments to redirect their learning. Our understanding of feedback resists thinking of it as something that produces unpleasant, squawking sounds: rather it is a guidance system.

Our approach

How many essays, assignments, reports have you marked? Unless you are new to higher education, the figure is likely to be in the thousands, so tutors reading this text are bringing a wealth of experience to issues about feedback. It is very difficult to stand back and think about something that has been standard practice. We probably all have our own way of marking and giving feedback to students. We are not saying that all current practice is wrong and we are going to put it right. Rather our approach is to share with you the results of our reading, research with students and reflection on feedback practices. We have been fortunate to have the time to do this, through Deirdre Burke's National Teacher Fellowship project and Jackie Pieterick's secondment to the Centre for Excellence in Teaching and Learning. Our involvements led us to consider our own practices on assessment and feedback, and stimulated us to move to a system that is more effective for us as tutors, but more importantly one that is more effective for student learning.

Jackie Pieterick, the author of Part I, 'Giving Students Written Feedback', has been teaching students on both sides of the Atlantic to write for over twenty years. Like many scholars and tutors trained in Rhetoric and Composition, she has an interest in higher education discourse communities, second-language acquisition and writing across the curriculum. She has received teaching scholarships at both undergraduate and graduate level, and in 2002 was awarded the School of Humanities, Languages and Social Sciences Outstanding Teacher Award. She founded the Creative and Professional Writing degree at the University of Wolverhampton, and is currently the School of Law, Social Sciences and Communication lead for the University's Centre of Excellence in Teaching and Learning. Her research on formative feedback, e-tutoring, first year experience and developing academic literacies across the curriculum has informed the numerous staff development training sessions she now runs for the University of Wolverhampton's Institute for Learning Enhancement (ILE). Jackie's interest in helping tutors learn to provide more effective feedback arises naturally out of the discipline of writing, where reading and responding to student texts is a frequent (and time-consuming) practice that can either motivate writers or destroy their writing souls. She therefore sees feedback as perhaps the most important dialogue tutors can have with their students and recognizes that, unlike her, many tutors have not been given any formal training on how to provide effective written feedback to students.

Deirdre Burke, the author of Part II, 'The Reception of Feedback by Students', brings over thirty years experience of teaching in schools and lecturing in higher education. Her primary focus in higher education has been subject teaching in Religious Studies, but she was extensively involved in initial teacher education for primary and secondary RE. She fulfilled cross-school roles in student support and development, which involved monitoring student learning needs, the identification of skill gaps, and the development of strategies to support student learning. She is also involved in the work of the ILE, and fed into initial developments in the Centre of Excellence for Teaching and Learning. More recently she has drawn on ILE staff expertise in student support, curriculum and technology to support her National Teacher Fellowship project on 'Getting more out of tutor feedback'. Deirdre's focus in Part II is on student use of tutor feedback as this has been the main thrust of her research on feedback since the late 1990s. However, as several of the case studies demonstrate, many strategies to help students get more out of feedback actually involve developments in the tutor provision of feedback. In addition, this section goes beyond subject tutors to identify the important contribution that staff in a range of institutional roles make to student use of feedback for learning.

Thus, the text is aimed at all higher education staff involved in the teaching and support of student learning. There are activities for you to use to develop your understanding of feedback and to develop your practice, and a range of activities designed for students to help them get more out of your feedback. Many of these activities are fleshed out in Chapter 9 in the case studies, to provide more extensive coverage and consider the benefits and challenges for each case.

Practical approaches

The aim of this text is to be flexible and to cover the range of understandings of feedback that tutors bring to their practice.

Is there a right way and a wrong way to provide feedback on an essay? How much feedback should you provide? Can you provide too much? There are obviously some aspects of feedback that we would have expectations about: notations must be accurate and the grade awarded should relate to assessment criteria. Other than these specifications, can we identify other aspects of written feedback practice as right or wrong?

Our intention is to provide a text based on extensive research of theoretical and action research on feedback issues in higher education, a text that explores key issues and allows you as a professional tutor to draw on aspects to inform your own practices – adapting and selecting as is appropriate for your own situation.

We aim to bring to your attention ways of providing feedback that make the process more effective for you as a tutor, by clarifying your purpose and illustrating ways to simplify the provision of feedback. Many of the case studies show how technology has been harnessed for feedback purposes, which either aim to simplify the process for tutors or expand the information provided for student learning.

We are aware that excellent tutor written feedback, while a suitable aim, is not an end in itself, as it does not automatically make feedback 'effective for the learner'. The other side of the equation is student use of the feedback to inform their learning. Just as tutors have largely been left to work out how to write feedback on student work, so have students been left to work out what to do with the feedback. Our approach holds that there are two essential steps in making written feedback more effective. First, tutors need to develop their awareness of issues surrounding the provision of feedback so that the feedback provided is more appropriate for student learning. That is not to say there is one way to provide feedback, rather a clearer understanding of your practice in the provision of feedback will make your feedback more consistent. The second step requires tutors to prepare their students for feedback and to help them develop strategies to unpack and act on tutor feedback. Consider the following examples:

- Example 1. My feedback practice is to focus on the assessment criteria for the task and to only comment on aspects of student work that engage with subject learning. If I see problems with grammar, I will suggest that students consult a skills advisor, but I will not point out errors.
- Example 2. My feedback practice is to mark all aspects of student work, to point out all errors in subject content, argument and grammar. I do this because I feel that if students are not made aware of spelling and grammatical errors they will think what they have done is correct. Correct grammatical presentation of work is equally important as the subject content of an essay.

In both these examples the feedback provided can be effective for student learning, as students are told what to expect and be guided in what to do with it.

A timely publication

The UK sector framework for our approach to feedback is provided by the Quality Assurance Agency (QAA) Code of Practice (6) for assessment of students. Sections concerning student learning, feedback and staff development provide sector expectations in relation to the design of assessment tasks, preparation of students, the provision of feedback, and finally guiding students to reflect and act on tutor feedback comments.

The publication of this text in 2010 is significant as this was the year for the Government target of 50 per cent of 18–30-year-olds to be in higher education to be achieved. This increase has two implications for tutors: first, increased class sizes, and second, the likelihood that these classes will present a wider range of learning abilities. Thus, our text explores ways to simplify the process of feeding back to large groups of students, and suggests ways to help students learn more from this feedback.

Additionally, the 2011 Higher Education Achievement Report will make transparent actual student achievement by listing grades for every module. The time of publication is also significant in relation to the continued development of education as a consumer product. On the one hand, we face the challenge of meeting students' expectations for the service we provide. This challenge is gradually being met in relation to student satisfaction in increased levels of satisfaction on tutor feedback, as indicated by the National Student Survey. On the other hand, the fact that students may regard education as a service they are paying for can be used to our advantage. Higgins et al. (2001) advised that tutors use this 'consumer awareness' to help students develop a better understanding of the place that feedback has in their learning. Irons showed agreement with this practice in his suggestion that we let 'students know that they are paying for the feedback – so they should use it' (2008: 46).

Hounsell's article on 'sustainable feedback' was a major stimulus to us in conceiving this text. We too seek to 'restore the position of feedback as a pedagogic resource that was prized' (Hounsell 2007: 103) and agree with the key ingredients to achieve this as high quality feedback and greater student involvement. Our extensive reading, research and reflection on feedback also lead us to agree with Hounsell that 'expertise in feedback – accomplishment in learning from and with it, and in being skilled at deploying it constructively – would itself become an outcome of higher education' (Hounsell 2007: 110).

Activities and case studies

Central to our approach are a range of reflective and/or practical activities. These activities aim to help you look again at feedback practices that you take for granted. Many of us followed a chain of transmission in writing feedback, being guided by the feedback we received as students. However, academic assumptions and practices that worked well in the twentieth century are under scrutiny as we face new constituencies of students, new approaches to learning and teaching and new technologies to underpin the assessment process. The activities aim to help you stand back and reflect on the assumptions you hold about feedback, and to explore your practices in the light of research on student views on feedback.

The majority of activities are designed for tutors to either reflect on their own practice or to use with students. Many activities were developed out of our work with students to make our feedback more useful for them, while other activities have been adapted from published works. Staff developers can use the list of activities to select tasks for staff development sessions, or work from the case study chapter (9) which sets out a range of activities in detail, considering the benefits for student learning, and the challenges in implementation.

Part I

Giving students written feedback

Dominating most past and present research on written commentary is the assumption that feedback on student compositions has a profound and positive effect on student revisions. This section introduces you to feedback from a tutor perspective, including ways of conceptualizing feedback in the context of educational and institutional reforms and ways of responding to students that move them towards both learning improvement and self-regulation. It begins by looking at the history of feedback research, from Thorndike's Law of Effect and Skinner's behaviourist approach to learning to cognitive-based research in the late 1960s and early 1970s to the new-millennial shift towards feedback for learning. It provides a brief overview of feedback research from a learning perspective, which emphasizes response practices and pedagogical thinking that is student-centred rather than text- or teacher-centred, and considers how composition-based research on feedback can equally inform our feedback practices.

The second chapter focuses on tutors' written comments as texts. It begins with a consideration of professional and personal issues, ranging from confusion about feedback purpose caused by conflicting definitions to the reading demands placed on us by student text, which can impact on our capacity to provide effective feedback. It contends that by broadening our notion of response and acknowledging the many and varied ways that we respond to student writing – as well as the many and varied ways that students influence and interpret those responses – we are more able to narrow the gap between our feedback practices and students' ability to improve their writing and learning.

Nearly all the research agrees that while commenting is a way of guiding a student to another writing and thinking level, tutors must be cautious about the control they assert over students' texts and the ways they choose to comment. That is, because tutors shape writers, they need to understand that not all commenting is useful and some comments may even be damaging. The third chapter encourages tutors to examine their comments' likely effects on writing and how their response styles reflect approaches to teaching and learning. It uses a series of cascading activities to guide this examination and offers examples of the various types of feedback comments that should be avoided and those we should embrace.

The final chapter in this section explores how constructive alignment, a term coined by John Biggs (1999), is one of the most influential ideas in higher education and can be used to guide tutor feedback and encourage more self-regulated learning in our students. It discusses how Biggs's model of constructive alignment can be extended to feedback through the use of criterion-referenced instructional rubrics and suggests strategies for constructing written commentary on students' work that is aligned with achievement of learning outcomes. It also offers samples of rubrics and constructively aligned criteria that can be shared with students through peer review and self-assessment activities, which both help students learn to close the gap between their performance and the learning goals and encourage them to become more self-regulated learners.

Although this section intends to move our feedback practices towards helping students improve both their performance and learning, it needs to be pointed out that because it focuses on comments provided by tutors to students, from the 'expert' to the 'apprentice', it necessarily relies on a transmission model of learning. However, because this section also offers advice about ways of making our written commentary more facilitative and useful so that students can hopefully develop new learning and make more intimate connections between what they learn, how they learn and why they learn, its theoretical underpinning is grounded in constructivist approaches to teaching and learning.

1

Overview of feedback research
A small sample of what's out there

This chapter offers brief summaries of research relevant to laying a foundational understanding of feedback from a tutor perspective and in the wider context of this book. It is highly selective and limited rather than comprehensive, preferring to focus on only a few works that have reviewed the extensive body of literature or conducted important empirical research on feedback in order to construct models of good practice. This overview will trace the ways thinking about feedback have evolved in order to demonstrate how we are currently theorizing and conceptualizing feedback in higher education.

Paradigm shifts • Feedback for learning • Drawing conclusions from educational theories • Feedback on writing • Drawing conclusions from composition theories • An overview of effective feedback • Recommended follow-up reading

In 1977, Marzano and Arthur arrived at the rather pessimistic conclusion that '[f]or all practical purposes, commenting on student essays might just be an exercise in futility' (quoted in Knoblauch and Brannon 1981: 1). In the new millennium, we still wonder whether our feedback is effective, whether students understand it, whether they will act upon it to improve their writing and learning, whether they read it all. Although it is sometimes tempting to treat such quandaries as 'meaning of life' questions that can never be answered, we persist in pondering them. We persist because we believe feedback is important. In fact, 'giving learners feedback is just about the most important dimension of the work of teachers in post-compulsory education' (Race 2005: 97). This belief is what motivates us to (re)search our feedback practices and theoretical models for answers to the 'what works and works best' question. What follows offers a very brief overview of this research.

Paradigm shifts

Research on feedback has a long, well-documented history. The earliest studies of feedback date back to 1911 and Thorndike's Law of Effect, which viewed feedback as 'knowledge of the results and reinforcement of the right answer' (McKeachie 1974: 7). Thorndike's 'Laws of Learning' paved the way for the next wave of feedback research, which was spearheaded by B.F. Skinner. Skinner's (1958) study of programmed instruction added immediacy of feedback to Thorndike's Laws, and proposed taking learners through information in successive small steps, while providing hints that would shape learner behaviour and strengthen desired responses. Most research conducted at this time used Skinner's behavioural framework, which regarded feedback as both a reinforcer and a motivator.

By the early 1970s, though, researchers began to doubt the feedback-as-reinforcement view. Kulhavy and Wager (1993) point out that 10 years of research under this paradigm showed feedback had no systematic effect on learning. As a result, research and theoretical models shifted towards an emphasis on process; on examining the basic functions of feedback in order to discover what was actually happening and how feedback influenced learners' cognitive and metacognitive processes. This conceptualization of feedback was grounded on the ways information is processed, and was rooted primarily in the position that tutors send students feedback messages about their strengths and weaknesses, which are then readily decoded and acted upon. What is significant about the information-process view is that it highlighted the informational role of feedback (Kulhavy and Stock 1989; Mory 1992). In many ways, current feedback research still builds on information-processing theory to determine the types of feedback that are most effective for learning, although there now appears to be a shift towards (re)conceptualizing learning from a constructivist perspective (Laurillard 2002; Nicol and Macfarlane-Dick 2006b).

The constructivist philosophy of learning postulates that knowledge is not external and therefore students must construct their own knowledge based on prior experiences, beliefs and ways of thinking (Duffy and Jonassen 1991; De Corte 1996; Nicol 1997). In other words, '[k]nowledge is constructed in the mind of the learner' (Bodner 1986: 873) and so each learner builds their own reality by interpreting experiences of the external world. The move towards a constructivist view of learning suggests that feedback will, in all likelihood, begin to function differently in learning environments, which is becoming evident in the linguist shift from talking about feedback *on* learning to feedback *for* learning.

Feedback for learning

The constructivist shift towards feedback for learning is evident in Ramaprasad's (1983) definition: information about the gap between actual performance level and the reference or standard level, which is subsequently used to alter that gap. Based on this definition, feedback for learning needs to be meaningful, understood and correctly acted upon. Thus, feedback for learning foregrounds the role of the learner in the feedback process. Educational theorists are therefore interested in not only contextualizing feedback and identifying the effectiveness of some types of feedback, but also in the ways students make meaning from their learning experiences and engage in self-regulated learning. Zimmerman and Schunk's (1989) *Self Regulated Learning and Academic Achievement: Theory, Research and Practice*, which addressed the practical applications of self-regulation in learning settings as well as individual self-regulating practices, has therefore been influential in guiding constructivist theories of feedback.

Indeed, recent synthesis of contemporary feedback models shows that they tend to frame feedback in the context of self-regulated learning. Butler and Winne (1995), for example, suggest that feedback be contextualized according to learners' prior knowledge and beliefs, which can provide insufficient information to affect knowledge construction. They propose a more elaborated examination of feedback that takes into account how feedback affects students' cognitive engagement with tasks as well as investigates the relationship between engagement and achievement. Butler and Winne identify feedback's potential roles in remedying students' failure to implement effective strategies and monitor their learning, and advocate that feedback should provide information about cognitive activities which promote learning.

At approximately the same time Butler and Winne were examining self-regulation and student engagement with feedback, Black and Wiliam (1998a) were reviewing research literature on formative assessment. Their analysis of hundreds of studies showed that formative assessment and feedback improved standards and learning. From their research, they concluded that learning improvement depends on five factors:

- providing effective feedback to students;
- students' active involvement in their own learning;
- recognizing the influence assessment (and by extension feedback) can have on students' motivation and self-esteem;
- students developing the ability to self-assess and understand how to improve;
- adjusting teaching to take into account assessment results.

They further suggested that feedback needs to help students recognize their next steps and how to take them, and should serve both social and managerial purposes rather than simply help students learn more effectively.

It needs to be pointed out that Black and Wiliam's work, as well as much contemporary research on formative feedback, is prefaced on Sadler's (1989) highly influential paper in which he identified three conditions for ensuring students benefited from the feedback they received:

1 students need to have some idea of goal or standard they are aiming for;
2 they need to be able to compare their actual performance with the desired goal or standard; and
3 they need to be able to close the gap between their performance and the desired goal by taking appropriate action.

Sadler also observed that students needed to have the same evaluative skills as their tutors in order to close any gaps in their performance. Nicol and Macfarlane-Dick (2006b) claim this observation has led writers like Boud (2000) and Yorke (2003) to conclude that tutors need to help students develop their self-assessment skills, as well as provide good quality feedback explaining how students can troubleshoot their own performance and take action to close the gap between intent and effect.

Many of the research and formative feedback models informed by Sadler tend to follow his lead and in some way associate self-regulated learning with performance. Dweck's (2000) research on belief systems and their relationship to motivation and achievement, however, raises a few questions about performance-based models. Her 30-year investigation has led her to identify differences between students who believe intelligence is innate and ability fixed and those who believe intelligence is malleable and ability dependent on effort. She concludes that such beliefs about intelligence orient students towards either performance goals or learning goals. That is, when students believe intelligence is a fixed trait, they tend to become overly concerned with performance goals because such goals validate their ability. In contrast, students who see their intellectual skills as something that can be developed and improved on through effort tend to be more concerned with cultivating their abilities than with how those abilities are evaluated. Dweck contends that these views can affect students' responses to difficulties they encounter in their learning, and she points out that performance-oriented students are less apt to persist when they fail than learning-oriented students. Similarly, Farr et al. (1993) also point out that learning orientation is character- ized by persistence and so learning-oriented students overcome failure to develop new skills and to use more complex strategies than performance- oriented students, who seek evaluation of their competence from others. Such findings seem to wave a cautionary yellow flag about performance-related feedback since it may not always help change students' attitudes and approaches to learning or ensure persistence, and could even reinforce 'grade- grubbing' in some students (Elliot and Dweck 1988).

Dempsey et al.'s (1993) work is considered one of the most comprehensive treatments of written feedback because it integrates feedback complexity, error correction and factors that influence learner confidence. Their model proposes an understanding of written feedback as a process that is made up of three cycles. Each cycle serves as a teaching and learning episode and together they form a framework for a formative process that leads to more successful task completion and enhanced learning. In the first cycle, students are presented with a task they need to respond to. Learners present their response to the task and receive feedback on it in the second cycle. The feedback informs the student about gaps in knowledge or performance and is then used to respond to the original task, which is presented again as a test item in the third cycle. Each cycle involves a series of steps that scaffold student performance and learning: input (from the task at hand to the learner), comparison (to some sort of standard or goal), and output (results). Dempsey et al.'s process model not only highlights the formative, interactive nature of feedback, but also the importance of timing feedback to promote usability and learning. According to them, delaying feedback in many instructional contexts 'is tan- tamount to withholding information from the learner that the learner can use' (1993: 24). Because Dempsey et al.'s model places emphasis on timing and a 'try-again' process, it has informed e-learning as well as classroom feedback practices.

Hattie and Timperley (2007: 88) reviewed all the works mentioned thus far, and numerous others, to propose a model of feedback that focuses on its purpose, meaning and potential to enhance learning. They suggest three 'feedback questions' that tutors can use: the first two ('Where am I going?' and 'How am I going?') provide performance-related information while the third ('Where next?') shifts away from performance towards self-regulation by offer- ing students the opportunity to consider 'learning possibilities for themselves'. Hattie and Timperley's model also identifies how feedback can focus on four levels:

- feedback focused on the task (e.g. provides information about the answer's correctness or offers guidance about obtaining more information);
- feedback focused on the process (e.g. information about the strategies used to approach and complete the task as well as suggesting alternative approaches);

- feedback about self-regulation (e.g. might comment on self-confidence or encourage appropriate help-seeking behaviour);
- feedback about the person (e.g. the use of praise or negative criticism).

They conclude that the most effective feedback focuses on process and task, while comments about the person are least effective because they distract students' attention from their learning.

Another feedback model which merits consideration because it has become the cornerstone for the REAP project (Re-Engineering Assessment Practices in Scottish HE), SENLEF project (Student Enhanced Learning through Effective Feedback) and the CETL AfL (Centre for Excellence in Teaching & Learning in Assessment for Learning) as well as numerous teaching and learning strategies, is Nicol and Macfarlane-Dick's (2006b: 7–9) *Seven Principles of Good Feedback Practice*. Like others before them, Nicol and Macfarlane-Dick consider how feedback can be used to help students develop self-regulated learning, and argue for the importance of both internal and external feedback in moving, or scaffolding, students towards learning in a more self-regulated way. Based on their analysis and synthesis of the ever-growing body of literature about feedback, they proposed the following six ways to support effective student learning:

1 help students to clarify what good performance is (goals, criteria, standards);
2 help students to learn how to self-assess, direct their own learning and support the learning of others;
3 provide students with opportunities to act on feedback (i.e. to close the gap between current and desired performance);
4 provide high quality information to students about their learning;
5 support the development of learning communities;
6 encourage positive motivational beliefs and self-esteem.

Nicol and Macfarlane-Dick conclude that rather than providing students with simple encouragement and praise on their performance, tutors need to compose task-oriented feedback. They claim that feedback which focuses on the task is more effective because it is more relevant to students, and is therefore better appreciated by them and more apt to be acted upon. They posit that since students must interpret feedback, it becomes a vital part of the self-regulatory process.

Like Nicol and Macfarlane-Dick and Hattie and Timperley, Shute (2008) applies findings from her review of literature on formative feedback to generate guidelines for good feedback practices. Shute's work attempts to highlight feedback's complexity and to show how this complexity has led researchers to arrive at differing conclusions about what constitutes effective feedback. Her review of the literature, which sometimes reads like a Who's Who in feedback research, focuses on 'task-level feedback' and attempts to identify the features of effective formative feedback. According to Shute, task-level formative feedback should provide timely and specific feedback about students' responses to a particular task. Her research also suggests it should be non-evaluative, supportive, genuine and credible. She also notes that formative task-related feedback needs to take into account the learner's current level of understanding and ability, as well as interact with other variables such as aspects of the task. Shute's focus on task-based feedback encouraged her to hypothesize that feedback containing detailed information about a learner's task performance would have a positive effect on student learning. Her findings from the research, however, neither proves nor disproves her hypothesis, which leads her to conclude that there are too many findings and not enough consistent patterns in the results to arrive at any definitive conclusion. She concludes that 'although there is no simple answer to the "what feedback works" query, there are some preliminary guidelines that can be formulated based on the findings' (2008: 29) (see Table 1.1).

Table 1.1 Formative feedback: guidelines to enhance learning

Things to do	Things to avoid
1 Focus feedback on the task	1 Do not give normative comparisons
2 Provide elaborated feedback	2 Be cautious about providing overall grades
3 Present elaborated feedback in manageable units	3 Do not present feedback that discourages the learner or threatens the learner's self-esteem
4 Be specific and clear with feedback message	4 Use 'praise' sparingly
5 Keep feedback as simple as possible (based on learner needs and instructional constraints)	5 Try to avoid delivering feedback orally
6 Reduce uncertainty between performance and goals	6 Do not interrupt learner with feedback if the learner is actively engaged
7 Give unbiased, objective feedback, written or via computer	7 Avoid using progressive hints that always terminate with the correct answer
8 Promote a 'learning' (rather than performance) goal orientation via feedback	8 Do not limit the mode of feedback presentation to text, and consider visual or acoustic options
9 Provide feedback after learners have attempted a solution	9 Keep use of extensive error analyses and diagnosis to a minimum

Source: Adapted from Shute (2008: 177–81)

Drawing conclusions from educational theories

So, what can be inferred about feedback for learning from this (limited) sampling of contemporary research? Understood within the context of the constructivist theory of learning, feedback for learning is viewed as part of the scaffolding provided by tutors which enables students to learn and therefore it needs to be thought of as formative, as a way of feeding forward to improve learning. It helps learners become aware of any gaps that exist between their desired goal and their current knowledge, understanding or skill and guides them through actions necessary to obtain the goal. Therefore, the most helpful type of feedback focuses on the learning task; it provides specific comments about task-related performance and offers specific suggestions for improvement, as well as encourages students to focus their attention thoughtfully on the task and their approaches to it rather than on simply 'getting the right answer to get a good grade'. This type of feedback is appropriate for most learners, but may be particularly helpful to lower-achieving students because it emphasizes that students can improve as a result of effort rather than be doomed to low achievement due to some presumed lack of innate ability. Effective feedback also promotes self-regulated learning. It encourages intrinsic rather than extrinsic motivation, which in turn builds learner confidence and promotes a sense of control and ownership over learning. In this respect, then, feedback is *for* learning.

Feedback on writing

Lillis (2001) points out that student writing sits at the centre of teaching and learning in higher education and is the dominant way of assessing student performance, thus writing instruction research on feedback merits attention. This research is extremely broad and has looked at the myriad ways tutors read and respond to student writing, from the subjective dimensions of grading to the empirical examination of student error, so a comprehensive discussion of it would be overwhelming. Like the previous section, then, samples from the body of research on feedback about student writing will be offered to demonstrate ways of thinking about feedback for writing improvement.

Unsurprisingly, composition theories experienced similar paradigm shifts as educational theories and at roughly the same times. Early research into feedback on student writing viewed writing-as-product and so focused mainly on error corrections. As a result, feedback was understood as being necessarily directive. As in the field of education, the 1970s ushered in a change in thinking about writing-as-processes. Researchers like Emig (1977) and Graves (1983), asked questions about what the act of writing involved and what sorts of skills it required. Faigley (1986) identifies that two groups began to emerge from the process camp at that time: expressivists and cognitivists. Expressivists view writing and the writing process as 'an art, a creative act' (Berlin 1988: 484) and draw heavily upon the humanist belief in agency. Expressivist tutors, like Elbow (1973) and Murray (1968), are interested in writer voice and encouraging students to take power over their prose, and so tend to advocate a non-directive or facilitative approach to tutor feedback. Cognitivists, like Flower and Hayes (1980), focus on the writer's mental processes, on thinking and problem-solving strategies, and draw influence from the field of cognitive psychology. Cognitivists are also concerned with understanding how a sense of audience is developed in the writer's mind and so these tutors' feedback focuses primarily on helping students move from writer-based to reader-based prose and in using process-based strategies for developing writing.

In the late 1980s, compositionists became interested in ways constructivism could inform pedagogy and practice, and some moved towards thinking about writing as 'primarily a social act' (Bruffee 1986: 784). Grounded in constructivist philosophy, which is heavily influenced by poststructuralists such as Foucault and deconstructionists such as Derrida, social constructionism asserts that knowledge is socially created and so locates it outside the individual. Social constructionists, like Lunsford and Ede, view writing as being 'produced through dialogue, always open to question, and a marker of social, ideological, and textual relations' (Carino 1991: 126). Social constructionist research, which has been greatly expanded by academic literacies researchers like Lea and Street, views writing and feedback as a social practice and so tends to focus questions about feedback on notions of discourse communities and writer identity.

Perhaps the most significant difference between the compositionists and educationalists is that since the idea of writing-as-process was first introduced, formative feedback has been an important element in writing instruction. Writing tutors have understood feedback as a way to feed forward since the 1970s. As a result, a substantial body of research on tutor feedback has been amassed. Although most past composition research into feedback on student writing tended to foreground the tutors' perspective, more recently there has been increased interest in exploring student writers' perspectives on feedback (Ferris 1995; Straub 1997, 2000; Lea and Street 2000).

Sommers' 'Responding to student writing' and Brannon and Knoblauch's 'On students' rights to their own texts: a model of teacher response' were companion research articles published in 1982. These landmark essays have been highly influential and had a long-lasting effect on the ways feedback has been understood and approached in the field of composition. As a result, most of the research has focused on (1) tutors' styles of written commentary in order to address the problem of how much control tutors should exercise over students' texts; and (2) trying to determine at what point in the writing process tutors' feedback is most effective.

Brannon and Knoblauch are noted for their observations about the way tutor comments exercise control over students' writing and thinking. Brannon and Knoblauch argue that tutors impose their own 'ideal text' on the student's work, which ignores the student's intentions and purpose in writing. When tutors 'appropriate' a student's text in this way, they often focus more on making sentence level corrections to the work which, while well-intended, has the effect of showing students that their purposes are less important than the tutor's agenda (Brannon and Knoblauch 1982: 214). Further, this focus also compromises the tutor's ability to help students articulate their ideas on the page and impedes their ability to recognize students' diverse ways of thinking and using language. Brannon and Knoblauch claim that tutors' feedback needs to draw a writer's attention to the relationship between intention and effect, not to explicitly tell the student what to do. This not only enables students to see the discrepancies in their texts, but also leaves final decisions about alternative choices up to the writer, not the tutor (1982: 162). Brannon and Knoblauch acknowledge that student writing must be evaluated at some point, but argue this should only occur after the writer has received peer and tutor feedback and had the opportunity to revise accordingly (1982: 221). They encourage tutors to adopt feedback practices that motivate students to make choices with their writing, which allows students to regain control over their texts. Brannon and Knoblauch suggest that tutors' responses should be structured as a dialogue between student and tutor about how the text can be revised to best achieve the student's intention. Tutors are thus seen as less restrictive, allowing students to experiment with their own thinking and writing processes.

Sommers (1982: 155) argues that, '[t]he key to successful commenting is to have what is said in the comments and what is done in the classroom mutually reinforce and enrich each other'. Her advice suggests that attempts to improve our commenting styles should integrate written comments with other pedagogical practices; we should make sure that written comments and other activities that structure writing complement rather than subvert the other's efforts. Like Brannon and Knoblauch, Sommers argues that teachers appropriate their students' texts by directing students to focus on areas that the teacher – rather than the student – deems important, such as grammar, word choice and style, which gives students an exaggerated idea of these elements' importance. More disastrously, Sommers' research showed that tutors' comments often give contradictory messages or are so vague that they 'could be interchanged, rubber-stamped, from text to text' (1982: 152). In 'Across the drafts' (2006: 250), Sommers returns to her earlier interest in response research and discusses the findings of a four-year longitudinal study. Sommers claims that 'most comments, unfortunately, do not move students forward as writers because they underwhelm or overwhelm them, going unread and unused' (p. 250). She reports that nearly 90 per cent of the students in the study wanted more specific feedback, suggesting that there is still a tendency for tutors to give students 'rubber-stamped' comments. She arrives at the conclusion that 'feedback plays a leading role in undergraduate writing development when, but only when, students and teachers create a partnership through feedback – a transaction in which teachers engage with their students by treating them as apprentice scholars, offering honest critique paired with instruction' (p. 250).

Straub's practical and empirical research (1996, 1997, 2000) on tutors' written commentary has inspired a renewed interest in writing tutors to reflect on the types and purposes of their feedback and to explore ways their feedback can improve student writing. Straub's (1997) study analysed the purpose and focus of tutor comments that first-year university students thought were most helpful in their efforts to improve their writing. His analysis showed that students in this study generally agreed that two types of comments are helpful: (1) comments that suggest ways of making improvements, and (2) comments that explain why something is good or bad in their writing. More specifically, the study also revealed the following:

- They preferred teacher comments that were stated clearly and explicitly.
- They also showed a preference for praise and open questions over criticism and closed questions.
- They felt that comments providing suggestions for improving (particularly those addressing organization and development of their writing) were helpful.
- They also preferred specific, elaborated comments.
- They appreciated having errors flagged up, especially if accompanied with recommendations for ways of improving their writing.
- They do not find 'traditional teacher responses' (1997: 94), such as editing symbols, abbreviations, cryptic marks and comments helpful.
- 'They were sensitive about comments on the quality of their ideas and resisted comments that [dealt] with matters that [went] beyond the scope of the ideas that they [had] on the page' (1997: 111) and were therefore wary of comments that criticized or questioned their ideas.

Straub's analysis encouraged him to conclude that 'well designed teacher comments can help develop students as writers' (1997: 92).

Ferris's goal in *Response to Student Writing: Implications for Second Language Students* (2003) is to trace, review and analyse second language (L2) writing research from a wide range of sources and to map out practical methods for responding to student writing. Although she sees a lack of consistent and reliable research dealing with second-language writing and the nature and effects of teacher feedback, Ferris suggests that written (and oral) teacher commentary, error correction and peer response produce beneficial results. Based on Ferris's research, the following can be concluded:

- Teacher commentary, whether direct or indirect, encourages and helps students improve their writing.
- Like many native speakers, L2 students are able to digest global and local feedback simultaneously because form and content are not separate entities and influence each other.
- More feedback on grammar is needed with L2 students because correct grammar does not come naturally over time (contrary to what some researchers believe).

- Offering indirect feedback on error correction may be impossible because of the teacher's role as authority/expert, and so all error feedback is necessarily direct.
- Students will improve over time if they are given *appropriate* error correction.
- Feedback given in the form of peer review can improve student writing so long as students are properly trained in ways that offer useful responses.

Because of the growing number of international students in higher education, it is important for tutors to be aware that although they must show consistency across marking, they need to address surface-level errors more rigorously with their L2 students if they hope to move them on to greater fluency and confidence.

Lea and Street's (1998) work on using an academic literacies approach to writing instruction has been highly influential in UK higher education research and scholarship, and much of the recent literature has adopted this approach by locating student writing within a social, political and institutional framework (e.g. Baynham 2000; Lillis 2001). Lea and Street's academic literacies approach stresses the need for students, faculty and others to acknowledge the fundamentally underdetermined forms and conventions of academic writing and to work together for greater transparency in giving and getting feedback.

Lea and Street contend that there are three main approaches to student writing and that tutors' feedback practices can be affected by the approach they adhere to:

- The study skills model looks at students' difficulty with writing as a deficit, which can be addressed through learning a set of skills.
- The 'academic socialization' model sees learning to write in higher education as a process of acculturation, which inducts the student into the institutional culture of the academy.
- The academic literacies approach views universities as sites of discourse and power, and sees academic practices as reflecting issues of identity and epistemology rather than simply skills or socialization.

Their later research (2000) on tutor feedback found that students had different interpretations and understandings of what they were meant to be doing in their writing and were limited in their approaches to writing. For example, Lea and Street's research shows that when students transferred writing strategies from one class to another, some students become unsuccessful and as a result receive negative feedback. Some students tend to approach writing as if is 'a kind of game, trying to work out the rules, not only for a field of study, a particular course or a particular assignment, but frequently for an individual tutor' (p. 42). As one of these students so tellingly says: 'The thing I'm finding most difficult . . . is moving from subject to subject and knowing how you're meant to write in each one . . . Everybody seems to want something different' (2000: 40–1). According to Lea and Street, except on a very general level of 'confidence' and 'practice', students often have little sense of cumulative progress in their development as academic writers. Their socially constructed definition of literacy moves student learning practices away from how tutors can help students to learn university literacies to how students and teachers understand the literacy practices of the university. They therefore advocate using non-judgemental comments and questions which attempt to enter into a dialogue with the student, rather than categorical statements and symbols which may be misunderstood.

Drawing conclusions from composition theories

Based on these examples of composition research, several conclusions can be drawn. Writing instructors and theorists all tend to assume that students will produce their writing through a process that provides them with feedback about how their texts are working on readers. Therefore students must have the opportunity to think and write in a scaffolded way, and tutor feedback serves a formative function throughout this composing process. Tutors need to adopt feedback commentary that encourages students to assume responsibility and control over their writing. These sorts of comments are more facilitative than directive; less judgemental, showing respect for students' writing as well as their ideas and beliefs; and offer specific information about where the writing has gone wrong and provide advice about how to improve it. Tutor feedback also needs to encourage students to see connections between and across modules, subjects and individual tutors, and engages them in an exploration and understanding of writing practices in the context of disciplinary and university discourse communities, which, like the world beyond the halls of academia, are never neutral and in a state of flux.

An overview of effective feedback

A model of feedback practice based on both educational theories and composition theories, then, would suggest that effective tutor commentary should attempt to do the following:

- Feedback needs to be formative, feeding forward to improve student learning and writing.
- Feedback needs to bridge the gap between performance and goals, between intention and purpose.
- Feedback needs to focus on the task and text.

- Feedback needs to be specific and provide advice about how to improve performance and writing.
- Feedback needs to promote self-regulated learning and writer autonomy.
- Feedback needs to encourage a dialogue between students and tutors about thinking and learning and writing and ways of knowing and ways of doing at university.

From a tutor perspective on feedback, then, our written comments need to move beyond a transmission model that assumes 'expert' control over the 'apprentice's' work and learning by either telling students what to do or pointing out and correcting errors. It needs to become more co-constructive and help them build on their learning experiences by contextualizing learning both in relation to current and future tasks as well as what's happening in the classroom; by guiding their own assessment of their work through well-wrought questions and comments that encourage them to 'fix things' independently and act on the feedback; and by actively engaging them in assessing and feeding back to each other in the classroom.

Recommended follow-up reading

Nicol, D. and Macfarlane-Dick, D. (2006b) *Rethinking Formative Assessment in HE: A Theoretical Model and Seven Principles of Good Feedback Practice.* http://tltt.strath.ac.uk/REAP/public/Resources/DN_SHE_Final.pdf (accessed 18 May 2010).

2

'Response-ability'
Feedback from a tutor perspective

This chapter will examine the roles of the tutor as reader, interpreter and evaluator of students' work to illuminate the complexity and problematic nature of responding to students. When tutors examine their approaches to reading and interpreting students' work and consider the kinds of responses they choose (or feel constrained) to use, they can begin to understand just how complex a task lies before them and to identify ways of managing it more effectively and efficiently.

Evaluative versus advisory feedback: the problem of clarity • Tutor roles • Tutors as readers • Feedback response-ability • Recommended follow- up reading

Think back to the first day of a class you took as an undergraduate; any one will do. You have the syllabus in front of you and while the tutor is busy dealing with students who have turned up in the wrong place, you decide to read it. Which sections do you give a passing glance to and which ones do you focus on closely? Do you quickly scan the weekly programme and reading list and then thumb through to the part about assessment? And when you read that the first assignment is a 1500-word essay due in week six, does your heart leap with unbounded joy? Do you think to yourself, 'I can hardly wait to start writing'?

Now fast forward to the present day and think about the last time you collected a batch of assignments. Did your heart once again leap with unbounded joy? Did you think to yourself, 'I can hardly wait to start grading'?

This scenario highlights the attitude towards assessment many tutors and students share. Assessment should be viewed as an opportunity to demonstrate and reflect on how much learning has taken place, but all too often it fills both students and tutors with dread and anxiety. From a student perspective, this dread can stem from performance anxiety, from a lack of confidence and from a fear of failure (e.g. Hembree 1988) and so assessment is fraught with self-doubt for many students, from beginning to end.

Tutors experience similar self-doubts. They wonder whether they are grading fairly, whether they will write the right comments, whether their standards are high enough or too high, whether they are striking the right balance between criticism and praise, whether they come across as too 'touchy feely' or too 'Stalinistic', and whether their comments will even be understood or used by students. Such self-doubt is further complicated by the fact that higher education (HE) tutors face considerable workloads, stoked by dwindling resources and increasing student numbers, and institutional processes such as semesterization and modularization, which all make it difficult for tutors to give quality feedback in a timely way that is useful to students. Many tutors also experience confusion over the purposes of feedback since the distinctions between formative and summative assessment are unclear (Black and Wiliam 1998b). This lack of clarity is more confounding because education reform documents and institutional policies present the two types of assessment as unproblematic and give little attention to 'the real features which differentiate the two' (Dixon and Williams 2001: 2). As a consequence, tutors are confused not only about the functions of formative and summative assessment (Harlen and James 1997), but also about the purpose and effect of the feedback they provide on these types of assessments. Tutors must ultimately bear the responsibility of evaluating and responding to their students' work, and this responsibility is impacted on by the tutors' attitudes towards their students, their professional disciplines, their jobs and their roles as readers of students' texts.

Evaluative versus advisory feedback: the problem of clarity

Because most assignments in HE tend to be summative, grading has come to represent the end of a learning process. In these sorts of end-of-module situations, feedback is often used to 'justify' the grade. And because grading is the object of so much anxiety, tutors want it done and over with as soon as possible so they tend to begin the process of reading student assignments as a process of grading. In fact, grading is what most tutors say they are doing from the outset: 'I'm grading essays.' Tutors' first impulse, then, is to approach giving feedback as evaluators, judges, critics or editors who go on a 'search and destroy mission' by launching a barrage of criticisms and corrections. Feedback is thus caught up in what Irons (2008: 8) calls the 'judgement culture associated with summative assessment'.

Although formative assessment and feedback have recently been a casualty of constrained resources in HE (Nicol 2007), their value in promoting learning is undisputed. As a result, they continue to reshape the ways tutors evaluate students and the way they think about feedback. For example, Wiggins (1997: 7) suggests that feedback should be reconceptualized in the following way:

> Feedback is a word we use unthinkingly and inaccurately. We smile at a student, say 'good job!' and call it feedback. We write 'B' at the top of a paper and consider it feedback . . . But feedback is something different. It is useful information about performance . . . it is not evaluation . . . Feedback is value-neutral help on worthy tasks. It describes what the learner did and did not do in relation to her goals. It is actionable information, and it empowers the student to make intelligent adjustments when she applies it to her next attempt to perform.

From this perspective, then, feedback should be targeted to enhance learning, concentrating on what to do to improve and ways to improve it, rather than aimed at evaluation. Wiggins, like numerous others, clearly distinguishes between feedback that advises and feedback that evaluates, which echoes Tunstall and Gipps' (1996) typology.

One important distinction often made between evaluative feedback and advisory feedback is that the former tends to be backwards-looking. Evaluative feedback gives a grade or rating – a snapshot or picture of the past – that captures the tutor's perception of the student's performance. It is given primarily to make sure the student clearly understands what the grade/rating/picture is for a task or assignment they have already completed – something that is in the past. This grade/rating/picture then serves as a reward or punishment for the student's performance. Advisory feedback, on the other hand, provides students with guidance about how to improve on future performances and as such is forward-looking. Its purpose is threefold: to provide learners with information about their performance in light of the task or assignment; to identify aspects of the performance which need improvement or support; and to improve student achievement by telling the learner what steps to take in order to move forward in the learning process. An example of how the two might look side by side is provided in Table 2.1.

Table 2.1 Evaluative versus advisory feedback

Advisory	Evaluative
• Provides evidence without interpretation or judgement • Describes the performance/product using only specific, concrete, non-judgmental language • Specifies context and goal (what/who/where/when/how)	• Provides a grade mark and/or expresses how well the tutor's instructional priorities have been met • Describes the performance/product using 'criterial' language (organized, polished, unpersuasive, unclear, etc.) and general words showing likes/dislikes • Praises and/or blames based on criteria
Commentary: Describe what happened in terms of the goal/standard. Confirm what was on-target to reinforce it and note what was off-target to underscore the need to reduce the gap between performance and goal/standard.	Commentary: Describe strengths and weakness of the performance/product in terms of the explicit (or implicit) criteria. Confirm what was valued by the reader.
Example: 'Your essay's conclusion bothered me because I felt like you wandered off on a completely different topic.'	Example: 'Your essay's conclusion was poor.'

Source: Adapted from Wiggins (2004)

Put succinctly, evaluative comments are judgements about the worth of the piece. Advisory comments provide information that leads students to make their own assessments of the effectiveness of their performance and are used by students to independently move to the next level of learning. Such distinctions would seem to imply that the two types of feedback are not to be considered different shades of the same colour.

Elbow (1993: 131–2, original emphasis), however, contends that evaluating is a crucial part of giving feedback to students. He describes it as:

> pointing out the strengths and weaknesses of different features or dimensions. We evaluate every time we write a comment on a paper or have a conversation about its value. Evaluation implies the recognition of different criteria or dimensions – and by implication different contexts and audiences for the same performance. Evaluation requires *going beyond* a first response that may be nothing but a kind of ranking ('I like it' or 'This is better than that'), and instead looking carefully enough at the performance . . . to make distinctions between parts or features or criteria.

Elbow describes the difference between feedback and evaluation in terms of might be called 'criterion-based feedback' and 'reader-based feedback'. The former asks 'What is its quality?' while the latter asks 'How does it work?'

For Elbow, evaluative comments focus on student performance, how well the student did in relation to criteria, rather than on grading or ranking the performance. Evaluative comments ask questions like: What are the strengths of this text? What are its weaknesses? What is the overall effectiveness and/or ineffectiveness of the text in relation to the set task? Its answer to the question? Its approach to answering the question? Its rhetorical purposes? In order for advisory feedback to describe the performance and make specific suggestions for what to do next, it too must ask similar questions.

So, while advisory feedback is seen to be at the opposite end of the feedback continuum to its evaluative counterpart in theory, the two overlap in practice. It appears, then, that the term evaluation has taken a confusing numerical turn from its original Latin meaning of 'to strengthen' or empower (Gitlin and Smyth 1989), and tutors would do well to remember that evaluation is not wholly about the measurement of things, about giving grades. It is, in fact, an integral part of feeding forward, which later chapters will show is important to students' self-efficacy and ability to use feedback effectively.

Although advisory and evaluative feedback are often seen as separate, the distinction is, in fact, blurred because evaluative feedback can play a forma-tive role (Orsmond et al. 2005). For example, a student's initial response to a low grade will, in all likelihood, be one of disappointment, but this may then be followed by a willingness to re-read the feedback and reflect on it. Additionally, distinctions between evaluative and advisory feedback can muddy the ways tutors actually go about giving feedback. For example, Elbow (1983) observes that tutors are compelled to play both judge and coach when responding to student texts. Yorke (2000: 496) explains that the reason tutors are compelled to inhabit such a double role is because at some point they have to switch from being 'supporter of learning to assessor of achievement'.

Tutor roles

One reason why responding to student assignments is taxing work for many tutors, then, is that it requires them to negotiate several different rhetorical and teaching purposes, which in turn asks them to inhabit different response personas. What roles and role adjustments do tutors adopt when reading and responding to students' work? And how does the role of tutor authority shape their responses?

Researchers tend to agree that tutors can assume a variety of roles when responding to student texts, acting sometimes as a judge, sometimes as a coach and sometimes as a typical reader (e.g. Dragga 1992; Fife and O'Neill 2001). Grant-Davie and Shapiro (1987) considered the metaphors used by com-position researchers to discuss tutors' reading processes and identified four roles based on feedback focus, purpose and when it occurs in the writing or learning process: judge, coach, doctor and intended reader. Purves (1984) doubles this and suggests tutors actually use eight personas when reading student texts (common reader, editor, reviewer, critic, proofreader, gatekeeper, anthropologist/linguist/psychologist and therapist), which are related to four general purposes in responding to student texts: to read and respond, to read and judge, to read and analyse and to read and improve. More recently, Tang (2000: 159) has adapted Purves's personas, deleting some roles while adding Reid's (1994) coach and discourse community expert and Knoblauch and Brannon's (1982) sounding board, to arrive at nine different roles tutors inhabit when reading and responding to student work. She describes how each one functions in the following way:

- Gatekeepers read the text to decide whether the student has sufficiently 'met some pre-determined criteria' in order to 'gain membership in some (presumably desirable) group'.
- Judges evaluate the quality of the text.
- Editors correct the text according to discourse and grammatical conventions.
- Coaches analyse the text and use their expert knowledge to encourage student improvement.
- Discourse community experts inform students about disciplinary expectations and conventions.
- Sounding boards enable the student to see gaps in the text and 'encourage the writer to explore alternatives that he or she may not have considered' (Brannon and Knoblauch 1982: 162).
- Collaborators work with students to produce the best quality work possible and provide feedback as a partner rather than expert.
- Conversation partners see feedback as interactional, as a way of creating a dialogue with the student.
- Common readers engage with the text 'out of pleasure and interest' (Purves 1984: 260).

What this suggests is that tutors not only have an extensive repertoire of personas to assume when offering feedback to students, but also that responding to students' work is a highly complex process that combines both formative and evaluative feedback. At the very least, then, giving feedback requires tutors to be schizophrenic because they must simultaneously enforce standards and nurture student learning – being at once judge and coach. And coaching, as Grant-Davie and Shapiro (1987: 3) point out, is equally as schizophrenic since tutors find themselves responding with the same sense of responsibility and helplessness as a football coach, cheering and chastising, 'while pacing the margins of their paper shouting tactical advice and encouragement'. It is little wonder, then, that giving students feedback is one of the most time-consuming and intellectually demanding duties tutors perform.

Activity: Which hats do you wear when responding to students' texts?

1 Consider Ramona Tang's nine tutor roles again and try writing a comment that each role might use in responding to students. For example, a Gatekeeper might write something along the lines of 'Your mastery of legal terminology indicates you are beginning to think more professionally, more like a solicitor.'
2 Did you find that some comments were easier for you to compose than others? If so, this might suggest that you have preferred roles when reading and responding.
3 Which new tutor roles would you consider inhabiting and which ones would you resist using the next time you respond to a student's text? Why or why not?
4 Which 'hats' are relevant for your subject?

Rest assured there is no single best reader role for tutors to assume when they read student writing. Often, tutors usefully assume more than a single role as they read and respond to a given assignment: the individual reader, the implied reader or target audience, the general or common reader, the teacher, the evaluator, the editor and the academic gatekeeper. Tutors and students both would benefit from tutors mastering a variety of types of responses to writing, including personal and empathetic responses, in addition to the traditional advisory and evaluative responses.

Tutors as readers

Tutors read (and re-read) as they mark papers. It is fair to estimate that for every hour tutors spend in the classroom teaching, they probably spend three times as many hours (or more) marking papers – three (or more) difficult, slow hours. In addition, when tutors read (and re-read) students' assignments, it is not for knowledge or for pleasure (although student texts can sometimes be pleasant – and humorously entertaining – to read). Tutors burning the midnight oil reading and responding to student papers, or packing stacks of assignments to take home for the weekend (or, worse yet, on holiday) frequently feel the onus of being the student's only reader and understand fully what it means to be a captive audience.

So reading students' texts becomes hard work. In fact, reading and responding to students' texts is exhausting work because tutors must concentrate intensely and must analyse, synthesize and interpret simultaneously. It is tiring work because tutors must also try to balance so many competing obligations and roles. They have an obligation to colleagues and their institution to follow shared standards and practices when giving feedback, and an obligation to their students to respond/critique/evaluate/motivate/advise (and sometimes even counsel) all at once.

Ede (1989) contends that tutors cannot help but recognize the complexity of reading and responding to students' work. They must begin by questioning their own predisposition to the texts they are about to read, including acknowledging that students have worked hard on those texts (very few students wake up in the morning and decide 'I'm going to write a rubbish essay today' and most sincerely believe that they have produced an 'okay' piece of work when they submit it). Quite often, tutors come to know cohorts of students and so the existence of real writers with whom the reader is acquainted creates a politically-charged reading environment that does not exist in other reading situations. Tutors therefore also need to keep an eye towards the kinds of comments they make as they read. As a result, tutors begin to feel they are 'walking a tightrope of conflicting demands' (1989: 155).

Generally speaking, all readers make assumptions about the texts they read. We can extend Grice's (1967) cooperative principles and identify the following as fundamental assumptions in ordinary reading situations:

- The text will not waste the reader's time (avoids waffling, wandering off the set topic and irrelevant information) or leave the reader confused.
- The writer will be honest (avoids writing something that lacks evidence or is false).
- The writer will have some authority on the subject (demonstrates knowledge and research).
- The text is well ordered and clearly presented (avoids ambiguity/obscurity).

But, as Lawson et al. (1989) point out, reading student-generated texts can rarely be considered an 'ordinary reading situation' and frequently these principles are turned on their head in the context of reading student writing. As a result, tutors always approach student texts with a good deal more scepticism than they do most other texts. Lawson and Ryan argue that the prospect of having to identify the weaknesses in a student text and then confront the writer with negative judgements can influence tutors as they interpret the text.

Additionally, what tutors think is going on in the classroom, the assignment, the text and the student affects how they read, what kind of audience they provide for the student and how they will respond. The way tutors read and respond to texts will ultimately impact on the way students write for them. According to Bazerman (1989: 142), how students perceive the tutor as audience will influence not only what students write, but also 'with what attitude and with what level of intensity'. Students' texts are thus strategic and stylized answers to 'questions posed by the situation in which they arose' (Burke 1967: 1). Usually, student-generated texts are the products of attempts to complete tutor-set assignments, which are then used for assessment purposes. Tutors' written comments are equally strategic and stylized responses to a situation, an assignment, a task, a question posed. As a result, tutors do not encounter student texts without encountering their students, themselves and the situation that generated the text in the first place.

Activity: Great expectations – how do you approach reading student texts?

Trace your response process, identifying how you approach the pile of scripts and each individual script.

- What happens as you read?
- Do you become immersed in the text?
- Do you fill in gaps?
- What types of personas do you assume?
- What are the preconceptions, constraints, routines and feelings you encounter when reading and responding to students?

Flynn and Schweickart (1986) advocate adopting a nurturing attitude that is coupled with high expectations, which helps students discover their own potential rather than demonstrates the tutor's power as expert. Because the tutor is always in the position of power and authority, students inevitably write assignments for the tutor, with the grader in mind. And because students see the tutor as their primary audience, it is the tutor's responsibility 'to draw the student into ever more ambitious problems and successful solutions' (Bazerman 1989: 143). In other words, 'response-ability' is the capacity to tease out what the students intended to do and help them understand how close they came to achieving their intended goals.

Bazerman (1989) suggests that one way to enhance tutor response-ability is to first read the situation – the kinds of learning and lessons students have been engaging with, the tasks set in the assignment, the student cohort and the tutor's own pedagogical stance. Once tutors have considered these fundamental issues, they then know what their reading goals are and what types of responses are most appropriate and useful for the student. He encourages tutors as readers to consider what roles they need to play in responding to this student on this assignment at this point in their learning experiences. They need to ask questions about whether they want to raise students' awareness of what has been achieved (or not achieved), and whether they want to remind students that something more is expected in both this task-related performance and future ones (for example, more breadth of research, fewer descriptive details or attention to grammatical propriety). When tutors know what they want to do, they know how to read and respond to the text. When they know what they want their feedback to do, they can read with an editor's helping hand, a proofreader's eagle eye, a grader's red pen or a professorial challenge.

To better consider the right level of response and how to position themselves as an effective responder, tutors can skim-read whole sets of papers before commenting on individual scripts. Skimming texts helps tutors to form a general impression, with an eye towards the sorts of comments the students need on a particular assignment and helps them to consider what responding roles they can adopt before re-reading and commenting. As they skim, tutors can ask these sorts of questions:

- What kind of reader does the text demand?
- What kind of reader does the tutor want to be?
- What kind of reader is best for the individual student?

The process of skimming also allows tutors to pile scripts together according to how successfully students have responded to and performed on the set task. In this way, they can work through the scripts without having to adopt new personas.

Another strategy is to assume the role of a reader-responder, which will help them resist slipping into the habit of giving the writer summative judgements on their work. The reader-responder assumes the role of intended audience in order to show the student how the text is working on a real reader, and therefore the tutor's intention is to guide rather than instruct, to respond rather than mark. By role playing students' intended audiences, tutors teach students that they are composing for an audience instead of 'performing for a verdict' (Elbow 1983: 225). This process of reading and responding is shown in Table 2.2.

Elbow's response style provides only enough ideas to think about what will nudge students to initiate certain lines of revision on their own, to engage them in making their own choices and developing their experiences as a writer. Tutors should therefore always reflect on how they can respond in ways that will lead to learning.

Another way to adopt reader-responses which provide students with effective formative feedback is to follow Rust's (2002: 153) advice:

- include a brief summary of your view of the assignment;
- relate specifically to the learning outcomes and assessment criteria;
- balance negative with positive comments;
- turn all criticism into positive suggestions;
- make general suggestions on how to go about the next assignment;
- ask questions which encourage reflection about the work;
- use informal, conversational language;
- explain all your comments;
- suggest follow-up work and references;
- suggest specific ways to improve this assignment;
- offer help with specific problems.

Table 2.2 Reader-based feedback guide

What was happening to you as you were reading?	*Summarize the text: give your understanding of what it says or what happened in it.*
1 What was happening to you as you read the first two paragraphs?	1 Summarize the text in thirty seconds. Let the writer hear you think out loud.
2 What words and phrases stuck out most?	2 Summarize the writing in a sentence, then a word.
3 What ideas, feelings, beliefs do you bring to this piece that influence the way you read it?	3 Summarize what you feel the student is trying but not quite managing to say.
4 What do you need or want as a reader? If you're fighting the piece or the writer, what would it take for you to go with the writer?	4 Summarize what you wish the text would say.
5 As you're reading, make marks to how you're reacting to the words; a straight line next to passages and words that work; a wiggly line for parts that bother you. Share these with the student.	5 What is this piece not about? What is the opposite of what it is saying?
6 Point to the passage that you appreciated, the ones you didn't understand or which made you stumble or resist.	

Source: Adapted from Elbow (1998: 256–63)

Feedback response-ability

Assessment and feedback are inescapable – for both students and tutors – and are part of a contractual agreement inherent in educational environments. In such environments, students agree to learn and have their learning assessed. In turn, tutors agree to assess and provide feedback on that learning. On the surface, then, giving and receiving feedback in any learning environment appears to be a fairly straightforward and predictable process. Yet this process is defined 'through implicit assumptions about what constitutes valid knowledge ... and the relationships of authority that exist around the communication of these assumptions' (Lea and Street 2000: 45). When understood this way, feedback is never neutral; it always carries highly charged messages about values and beliefs, about competence and identity (Ivanič et al. 2000), as Chapter 7 explores further in its discussion of Race's idea of 'uncompetence'.

Tutors therefore need to be sure about their purpose in reading and responding to students' work. They need to understand the distinctions and connections between traditional modes of commenting associated with summative and formative assessments because mixing up the two tends to keep them from noticing that they can get by with far less grading. And while having a repertoire of personas we can inhabit the next time we collect assignments will not make our hearts leap with unbounded joy (nor will it stop many of us from having immaculately clean cars and houses, meticulously manicured lawns and alphabetized wine racks), it will enhance our ability to give relevant, helpful feedback to students that is aligned with the type of feedback individuals will act on and recognizes where students are now . . . on this assignment at this stage in the process and at this point in their learning.

Recommended follow-up reading

Elbow, P. (1993) Ranking, evaluating, and liking: sorting out three forms of judgment. *College English*, 55(2): 187–206.

3

'Out of control'
Issues of control in tutor feedback

This chapter uses a series of cascading activities to encourage tutors to think about their response practices and to consider ways of improving them. It provides theoretical underpinning to offer practical strategies for making written feedback more effective and efficient.

How much feedback is enough? • Where is the best place to write comments on student texts? • What sorts of things should tutors focus their comments on? • What types of feedback styles work best? • How much praise (or blame) should we use? • Last words? • Recommended follow-up reading

In 1982, Sommers observed that despite the fact 'commenting on student writing is the most widely used method for responding to student writing, it is the least understood' (p. 148). Although she was referring to gaps in writing research in the late 1970s, Sommers' observation rings true for many tutors today. That is, tutors frequently provide students with written feedback, but quite often are uncertain about how it works – and why it doesn't. Even the most experienced tutors have lingering concerns about ways of responding efficiently, effectively and fairly to students' work. It makes sense, then, for tutors to examine their feedback practices and written commentary more closely. As Straub (1996: 248) suggests, 'All of us, it seems to me, would do well . . . to take a close, hard look at the comments we make, consider whether they are doing the kind of work we want them to do, and make whatever changes we can to make them work better.'

The following reflective activities are designed to help you analyse and evaluate your written commentary, and increase your awareness of the ways your current feedback practices can be aligned with contemporary feedback theory and pedagogy. By gaining a deeper understanding of our current feedback practices, we are better able to refine our comments to improve student learning and writing – without compromising response practices that are personally relevant. Reflective activities can be approached in a variety of ways. Some tutors may want to begin by identifying the areas of written response they feel less confident with. Others may want to select topics they believe would be most appropriate or useful for their learners. Alternatively, the activities could be approached sequentially. While the reflective activities explore tutors' feedback practices on students' written text, strategies suggested can be transferred to other types of assignments which require tutors' written commentary.

How much feedback is enough?

This activity asks you to reflect on the number of comments you make on scripts and how feedback volume can affect students' ability to effectively use comments.

Activity: The Goldilocks principle – how much feedback do you provide?

1 Using a student script that you have already responded to, count the number of comments you have made on the text. You should include comments made in margins, body (within the text's body and include 'comments' such as ticks and underlines) and at the end. End comments are counted as a single response, regardless of length.
2 How many comments did you make?
3 Now consider whether the number of comments on this script is representative of your typical response to student texts. Do you usually make fewer, or more, comments? If the number of comments on this script is not typical of the way you usually respond, what might account for the difference?

According to Brookhart (2008: 13) the Goldilocks principle is based on the saying, 'Not too much, not too little, but just right'. It is generally acknowledged in the feedback literature that a paper returned without any comments on it is perhaps the worst possible type of feedback students can receive because there is nothing to act on and therefore it does not improve their learning or writing. However, excessive tutor commentary can be equally problematic for students because there is simply too much to digest and act on, which is echoed later in Chapter 5's examination of what students say they want from tutor feedback. Although the number of comments tutors make on scripts varies case by case, especially when responding to English as a second language (ESL) writers, Straub's (1996) research suggests that the more comments a tutor makes on a student's text, the more controlling the tutor is likely to be. When tutors exert too much control in their feedback, they not only run the risk of appropriating student texts but they also redirect students' attention 'towards the teacher's purpose in commenting' (Sommers 1982: 149): the tutor assumes most of the responsibility for writing and learning rather than the student. The feedback stops being formative, and thus no longer helps students to become independent, critical thinkers and more self-regulated learners. In order to exert less control over student texts, and provide students with feedback that can be acted on, Ronald Lunsford (1997) suggests that fewer, more carefully designed comments are likely to be more effective than too many unfocused ones.

Although ambitious students are likely to read more of their tutor's feedback comments than students aiming only to get through, it is a good idea not to write any more on the paper than the student is going to read, understand and use, and to follow Lunsford's suggestion about designing comments so they are more effective. One strategy for responding that conserves time and provides relevant, useful feedback is the PQR system. The first comment praises what works and works well in the text. It is important that any praise offered is genuine, specific and usable, rather than acting as a 'bad blow cushion' for any criticism that follows. So rather than simply writing 'Great intro!' write, 'Your essay started off very well, with definitions and a clear, focused thesis', which identifies the features that make it effective and reinforces what the tutor expects to find in an introduction. The second comment presents questions related to gaps in the student's knowledge and the paper's argument or information for further consideration. It is worth bearing in mind, however, that students can sometimes read tutor's questions as rhetorical so it is usually better to formulate questions as comments. For example, rather than beginning with 'Why didn't you . . .' try starting with 'I was left wondering about these points . . .'. The final comment encourages the student to revise with specific advice about how to do this (e.g. 'Next time, check your paper in these ways . . .').

A similar strategy would be to use Hattie and Timperley's (2007) feedback questions as a guide. For example, on a draft or first attempt paper, formative feedback could be presented as three sentences that comment on what parts of the assignment the student has achieved ('Where am I going?'), what parts they need to work on ('How am I going?') and what steps are needed to fill the gap ('Where next?'). On a summative piece of work, the tutor could use the same strategy, but focus the last comment on how to carry knowledge and skills learned in the assignment forward to future learning tasks and suggest ways to improve them. This modification encourages tutors to include prognostic feedback, which aims to increase the value of feedback to the student by focusing comments on the future, on what they can do well and to do it better. More advice about helping students use this type of proactive feedback will be offered in Chapter 7.

Where is the best place to write comments on student texts?

This reflective activity asks you to consider your use of marginal, body and end comments.

Activity: Location, location, location – where do you comment on essays?

1 Return to your marked student script and consider where you are commenting this time.
2 Have you written any comments in the margins? If so, how many? Were any of them complete sentences? Did you write an end comment? What did you focus it on?
3 If most of your comments are marginal, why do you think you have responded this way? If you commented only at the end of the script, what prompted you to do this?

Research investigating how comment location is interpreted and used by students suggests both modes of marginal and end comments can be effective. Connors and Lunsford (1993) notice that while some tutors used a combination of terminal and marginal comments, others chose to use one or the other. Leki (1990) concludes that there is no conclusive evidence that either comment placement is more effective or preferable. Ferris and Hedgecock (1998) draw the same conclusion, but suggest that each may have advantages; there is usually more room to write end comments so they may be clearer, while marginal comments are more immediate and proximate. Pieterick's (2009) research shows that students are strategic in their approach to reading feedback comments. Most tend to read end comments first because they are believed to contain information that 'explains the grade' or 'tells me how I did'. They then read marginal comments for information they believe shows them specific places in the text where they 'got it wrong or right'. Her research suggests that, particularly in summative situations, students do not see either type of comment as learning tools.

Perhaps the most useful advice on comment location is provided by Hodges (1997). She suggests that margins can be used to create more intimacy and to demonstrate how tutors are reading the text. Her suggestion affords tutors the opportunity to strategically use marginal comments to emulate a kind of dialogue that shows the reader's intellectual engagement with the text and its ideas. Numerous feedback scholars advocate engaging students in a dialogue (Sadler 1989; Askew and Lodge 2000; Lea and Street 2000; Hounsell 2003, 2007; Nicol and Macfarlane-Dick 2006a) and therefore using marginal comments to show students that conversations about ideas and learning can take place in their own texts seems good advice. To avoid mismatched intentions, understanding and expectations, however, tutors need to explain – perhaps even demonstrate – to their students how to interpret and use marginal comments as a dialogue about their knowledge, skills and learning, and encourage them to 'talk back' by commenting on the comments. One way of demonstrating the dialogic nature of marginal comments is to have students submit their first written assignment as a two-column text, as suggested by Brannon and Knoblauch (1982) and demonstrated later in the first case study in Chapter 9.

The body of the paper is on the left side and the right side is used for a running commentary between tutor and student. The student uses the right margin to comment on his or her rhetorical intentions and authorial choices and submits it the tutor, who responds first to the paper's body and then to the student's comments. The text is then returned to the student, who responds to the tutor's comments and explains what changes he or she would make. The student then resubmits the paper for the tutor's evaluative response, which considers the student's revision strategies in feeding forward, and (sometimes) a grade. Not only does this strategy promote students' understanding of how to use marginal comments and guide them towards more self-regulated learning, it also helps the tutor identify more effective feedback for students since the students are showing how they are interpreting the comments and their approaches to learning and writing. Without this sort of coaching, however, students may simply see the tutor as a marker and thus interpret marginal comments as corrective and evaluative statements.

Hodges (1997: 81) also reminds tutors that their marginal comments need to have a clear relationship with the end comment: that is, comments in the margins should serve as 'trail markers' that lead to the end comment. One strategy tutors could use to align their marginal comments with their end comment is to refer their marginal comments back to specific criteria in the assignment. Because marginal comments direct students' attention to specific assignment issues in their papers, end comments, which tend to provide more evaluative information about task-related performance, will help students create a big picture of the smaller, marginal points. However, tutors should resist formulaic end comments that simply repeat assessment criteria in favour of those which are specific to the individual text and learner needs.

What sorts of things should tutors focus their comments on?

This activity is adapted from Sprinkle's (2004) reflective model for feedback. It encourages you to look at the types of features you emphasize in your comments on student texts and to consider how this focus directs student attention.

Activity: Auto-focus – what types of thing do you comment on?

1 Revisit the student script, or another one you have responded to previously, and number your feedback comments. Simply start at the beginning of the text and place sequential numbers next to each comment. For numbering purposes, comments should be distinguished from each other conceptually rather than semantically. This means that multiple sentence comments like end comments may need to be divided into several separate comments. Conversely, several sentences addressing the same theme may be considered one comment. Be sure to include any comments you made on assignment cover sheets or assessment rubrics.

2 Using the Features Focus Chart below, begin categorizing your numbered comments according to the feature headings (e.g. focus, mechanics, process). Simple hash marks (///) will do.

	Content features		Textual features		
Comment number	Focus		Development and support	Organization	Mechanics and style
1					
2					
3					
4					
5					
6					
etc.					

---

3 To help determine which category comments belong to, try using these examples:

• *Focus:* Comments or marks that address the paper's focus or adherence to a central point (e.g. 'You seem to drift from your main point in the middle of the second page' or 'Perhaps dealing with only two types of social inequality might be more manageable for you – and it will allow you to focus on each one enough to answer the assignment question.)

- *Development and support:* Comments that address the use of evidence from researched sources and other supporting devices such as quotations, examples, statistics, etc. (e.g. 'Can you provide a specific example here?' or 'Explaining more about this concept would help readers understand your ideas a bit better' or 'Your main points seem unevenly developed because you wrote six paragraphs more about operant psychology').
- *Organization:* Comments that address the paper's organization of ideas and information (e.g. 'On the third page you talk about public health education, move on to the NHS and then go back to public health education. Does this seem effective to you?' or 'Because it's so powerful, you might want to put this narrative at the beginning to grab the reader's attention').
- *Mechanics and style:* Comments, edits, minimal marks or correction symbols that attend to textual features such as punctuation, grammar, spelling, capitalization, the format of the essay, etc. (e.g. 'This 78-word sentence has too much information to digest in one go, so can you try to break it down into more manageable chunks for me?' or 'The Harvard system places dates and page numbers inside brackets' or 'Paragraphs are always longer than one sentence in academic essays').

4 Do you notice any patterns in your feedback focus? Are you making more comments about content? Or do your comments tend to focus more on textual features? Does this coincide with what you want the student to think about and focus on?

5 Now write a brief statement about your assignment purpose – what you wanted the student to learn from doing this assignment. Compare this statement with the way you ranked your comments. Do the features you emphasize match your assignment purpose?

Griffin (1982: 299) argues that 'the major question confronting any theory of responding ... is where we should focus our attention'. In student-centred learning, tutors first consider what students perceive as most important to their learning as a way of guiding feedback focus. It is fairly safe to say that most students – even the ones who go on to become writing tutors – do not enrol in higher education to learn how to write: they come to university to study a particular subject. Students therefore expect that the written assignments they submit will be assessed primarily on their discipline-specific knowledge. And although students know from past experience that tutors will also comment on the way they use sources, structure information and language, they expect most of their tutors' comments to focus on subject content and their ideas (Norton 1990). It can be assumed, then, that when a student's paper is returned with an unexpected number of comments about mechanics and language error, that student will be confused and disappointed, if not frustrated and angry.

According to Radecki and Swales (1988: 72), a tutor's time should be spent commenting on global concerns such as content and the meaning rather than on correcting grammar and punctuation. In fact, most subject tutors have more confidence and are more interested in providing feedback to students on their content (Beason 1993). Connors and Lunsford's (1993) study found that the most common types of tutor comments were content related, and focused on the effectiveness or lack of supporting details, evidence and examples. However, Storch and Tapper's (2000) research highlight that tutors' comments are not always aligned with the assignment purpose. They found that while assignments tend to stress content, the frequency of tutors' content comments did not always mirror this emphasis and focused on other features, such as mechanics and sources, in equal or greater proportion. For example, a tutor might set an assignment which intends to have students examine the arguments surrounding capital punishment and to develop fluency with legal discourse. However, if that teacher then makes more comments on sentence structure than content matters, there could be an imbalance between feedback and purposes. Other studies on tutor comments also show there is a tendency for tutors to focus (consciously or unconsciously) on textual errors related to grammar and structure (e.g. Zamel 1985). Connors and Lunsford (1993) suggest that tutors make numerous surface level error corrections because they are easy to do while reading, which suggests most tutors' intentions in commenting on these types of errors attempt to show students how their writing obstructs meaning and impedes reading – how they are communicating their ideas. Because tutors attend to numerous types of surface-level errors, this conflicts with students' expectations that they will receive more comments about content. As a result, many students come to think that error-related feedback suggests they need to focus more on 'fixing' their language than on developing their ideas (De Beaugrande 1979; Ashwell 2000).

There are numerous strategies tutors can use to create greater balance between their content and textual comments' focus. Rather than correcting or noting *all* errors of style or grammar as they read, which only serves to show the reader's annoyance and prevents students from taking responsibility for self-editing, identify one or two examples in the text where the student has written something articulately (or at least 'articulately' for that particular student). These examples can then be referred back to as self-generated models which show the students they are capable of having facility with words in an academic context. Students can then be directed to a part in the text where meaning was obscured or language was confusing and told to compare the two examples. Tell them to try re-crafting the 'bad' example so it reads more like the 'good' one in order to train themselves to write more clearly and fluently in their future assignments. Another way to prevent over-correcting is to read the text for patterns of error. Pointing out two or three *kinds* of error can show the need to focus revisions and writing for other assignments on the types of things that keep readers from paying attention to the paper's content. Then refer students to sources which will help them understand these patterns and give them advice on how to 'fix the problem'. One advantage to reading for patterns of errors is that many students frequently make similar types of errors. Rather than write the same comments and advice on every student's script, it is much easier to feedback information about errors to an entire class. Remember, though, that ESL students will want and expect more corrections and advice about grammar and language use (Leki 1991; Rennie 2000).

What types of feedback styles work best?

The types of comments tutors use can impact on students' ways of learning and their motivation. The 'out of control' activity asks you to examine whether your feedback style is directive, facilitative or a combination of both, and to consider how these two types of comment function.

Activity: Out of control – how much control do your comments exert over the student's text?

1 Following the same instructions as provided in the 'Auto-focus' activity (see p. 42), this time begin categorizing your feedback comments using the following table (adapted from Sprinkle (2004) and based on Straub (1996)).

Number of comments	Directive (explicit comments about specific changes particular to the text)			Facilitative (observations intended to engage writer with work more critically)		
	Corrections	Commands	Evaluations	Suggestions	Questions	Reader response
1						
2						
3						
4						
5						
6						
etc.						

2 To help determine which category comments belong to, consider their perceived intention and try using these examples as a general guideline:

- *Corrections:* Comments or marks that correct content or indicate mechanical errors. Minimal marking, correction symbols, and editing are included in this category (e.g. 'You're referring to "intonation" rather than "accents" here').
- *Commands:* Comments that tell the reader exactly what to do or write (e.g. 'Explain the new programme more' or 'State your thesis at the beginning rather than at the end of your essay' or 'Move this to the second paragraph').
- *Qualified evaluations:* Comments that use qualifiers to temper the tutor's authority and imply less control (e.g. 'This *seems* a little too general and *perhaps* unrealistic').
- *Advice/suggestions:* Comments that suggest editorial changes or further research (e.g. 'At this point, you could try outlining your major points and restructuring your report to fit that outline' or 'Deirdre Burke discusses this idea in her article on feedback, so you might want to have a look at what she says' or 'I'd suggest reworking this paragraph').
- *Reader response:* Comments that reflect an understanding of the writer's purpose or engagement with the topic, or that attempt to create identification with the writer, or that attempt to show how the text is working on the reader (e.g. 'Your interest in tort law really shines through in this part because your ideas are so clear' or 'I find this a very original and thought-provoking point!' or 'You're starting to lose my attention at this point').
- *Questions:* Comments that ask real (rather than rhetorical) questions (e.g. 'Are you sure this is a true statement?' or 'How might you refute a counter-argument for this?' or 'If you were a debt counsellor, would you recommend liquidation to the client?').

3 Now look at where most of your comments are located on the table. Do you tend to be directive? Facilitative? Is there a fairly equal balance between the types of comments you use?

According to Black and Wiliam (1998a), two main functions of feedback are to be directive and facilitative. Directive feedback, such as evaluative and instructional comments, tells the student specifically what needs to be fixed or changed. Facilitative feedback (sometimes called the 'Rogerian technique') is based on asking questions and making suggestions for further consideration. Providing cues and guidance through facilitative feedback is conducive to students' ability to clarify their thoughts and approaches to learning, while the corrective information contained in directive comments shows students precisely what they need to do to improve performance and moves them closer to the correct answer.

Straub (1997: 223) points out that recent scholarship on written commentary has 'urged us to reject styles that take control over student texts and encouraged us instead to adopt [feedback] styles that allow students to retain greater responsibility'. Because the types of comments tutors make can exert control of the students' texts and ideas Straub argues that tutors can obstruct learning when they exercise too much control through their comments (Straub 1996; Fedor et al. 2001). Grant-Davie and Shapiro (1987) advise tutors to think about their purposes for feedback comments, and to use them to teach students to become their own best readers. To achieve this goal, tutors should respond with more questions and suggestions and fewer judgments and directives. According to researchers who advocate the use of facilitative feedback, these non-evaluative comments tend to initiate a more direct response from students because they are required to think about their ideas and the changes they make instead of simply following the tutor's 'orders'. When tutors provide comments in the form of ideas, opinions and suggestions that portray them as interested readers, the comment style becomes more learner-centred and promotes autonomous learning.

Although facilitative comments tend to promote more self-regulated learning, they can also be problematic for students. Spandel and Stiggins (1990) argue that students frequently misread tutors' comments and thus fail when trying to make changes. As Chapter 5 will demonstrate clearly, students do not always understand tutors' feedback comments (Chanock 2000; Nicol and Macfarlane-Dick 2006b). Therefore they do not always know what to do with the facilitative questions and reader responses offered in their texts. For example, students can read tutor questions as rhetorical rather than as genuine or pedagogical ones that point to gaps in knowledge/information or discrepancies in the text. Many students, especially those first entering higher education or just learning a topic or content area (e.g. Knoblauch and Brannon 1981; Moreno 2004), still need step-by-step support in order to make necessary changes to their knowledge and writing, and so benefit greatly from more directive written comments. They need specific comments about errors and specific suggestions for improvement, which encourage them to focus their attention thoughtfully on the task rather than on simply getting the right answer (Elawar and Corno 1985; Bangert-Drowns et al. 1991). However, research by Chinn and Brewer (1993) suggests that some students will reject or devalue corrective feedback in order to protect the integrity of their knowledge and beliefs.

Facilitative and directive approaches are by no means mutually exclusive. As Straub (1997) points out, tutors would do well to work on developing a fairly balanced style of commenting that refrains from exerting a high degree of control and at the same time recognizes that autonomy does not mean students are left to learn completely on their own. Creating a balance between facilitative and directive comments promotes attention to task performance and students' ability to self-regulate by making choices (which may or may not be provided by tutors). It can also demonstrate respect for students' individual approaches to writing and learning by shifting the balance more towards the use of one type of comment.

Decisions about how much directive or facilitative commentary to use, then, are almost always contextualized by the larger goals of the assignment and learning outcomes and based on the students' level of learning. One way of approaching these decisions is to take stock of where the students are in the learning process by providing more directive comments on first year students' papers and then introducing more facilitative responses as they progress through semesters and levels. Another approach combines the two types in a single comment. For example, rather than responding with either 'Do more research on riparian vegetation' or 'What happens to riparian vegetation?' tutors could write 'You need to think about a dam's impact on riparian vegetation (directive), so where might you look for information on how plants along rivers are effected by damming (facilitative)?' These sorts of comments *specifically* tell the students what needs to be changed in relation to the set task and at the same time guides them towards how to make the changes without limiting choices. Additionally, comments like this define discipline-specific words which may be confusing for the student and assume the student *will* make the necessary changes to improve performance.

How much praise (or blame) should we use?

The activity 'The good, the bad and the effective' asks you to examine your feedback commentary to see if you tend to provide more positive than negative commentary since research suggests that both can impact on students' performance and motivation.

Activity: 'The good, the bad and the effective' – your use of positive and negative comments

1 Return to the marked script one last time. This time though, you will need to identify your positive and negative comments, marking the ones that praise (+) and those that criticize (–). One way to approach this is by looking for the strengths and weaknesses you commented on in the text.
2 How do you phrase positive comments? And how do you phrase negative ones? Do you use one word? Three words? Complete sentences? Do you explain why some things are good/strong and some are bad/weak? When you give students praise and criticism, do you see yourself assuming the role of coach or judge?
3 Consider these statements: 'We catch more flies with honey than vinegar' and 'It's always best to sugar the pill'. Do you think these statements ring true with regard to teacher feedback/comments? Why or why not? How might these ways of thinking promote student performance and motivation? How might they foster dependency on tutors and their feedback?

If tutors want to write commentary that serves the purpose of feedback *for* learning, Haines (2004: 19) says that they should 'increase [the] use of praise, and descriptive observation ... [and] take greater care with direct criticism' because giving students too many negative points can 'demotivate' them. However, tutors need to be aware of how they are using praise since it frequently only serves to soften the blow of criticisms and suggestions rather than responding to good work. Hyland (2001), for example, has noticed that numerous criticisms and suggestions offered in tutor commentary are mitigated through hedging, questions and personal attribution. She acknowledges that these types of mitigation strategies reduce the force of criticisms, but warns that such indirectness carries the potential for being misunderstood by students, who may see it as an estimate of their ability (Deci 1972) rather than commenting on their task-related performance.

Researchers tend to have differing views on the value of praise as a form of feedback. Sadler (1989) and Hattie (2001), for example, agree that praise has its place in the classroom, but do not see it as a valuable form of feedback. Podsakoff and Farh (1989: 62) noticed that when students receive negative feedback, they become dissatisfied with their performance level, set higher goals for future performance, and then perform at a higher level than students who receive positive feedback or no feedback at all. Butler (1987) and others suggest that use of praise as feedback directs the learner's attention to 'self', which distracts from the task and learning.

Praise, however, is seen to encourage students to overcome writing apprehension and motivates them to develop more positive attitudes. Numerous other researchers (Connors and Lunsford 1993; Bardine et al. 2000; Straub 2000) also feel that praise tempers students' apprehensions and motivates them, so they examined the frequency of teachers' use of praise. Straub, for example, learned that students do value praise and prefer it over criticism. Yet tutors are not always aware of this preference, as Connors and Lunsford's (1993) research revealed. Their study showed that teachers gave twice as many negative comments as they did positive ones. Additionally, tutors' positive comments tended to be given on A-graded papers and were the shortest and friendliest, and most followed their critiques of the work with positive commentary. Smith (1997: 262) also found that tutors alternated between praise and criticism, and typically praised things like effort or interest more than content and textual features. While this sort of praise may motivate students to 'keep trying', it does not provide them with any useful information about their performance, understanding or written communication. (Also see Chapter 7, which provides more advice on ways of helping students work with both positive and negative comments.)

Students might be pleased with the praise they receive, but they are not always sure what is 'excellent' or 'good' about the work. As a result, they may not be able to replicate its quality, which leads Race (2001: 69) to suggest that 'it is better to praise exactly what was very good or excellent in a little more detail, rather than take the short cut of just using the adjectives themselves'. In effective feedback, being positive means describing how the strengths in a student's work match the criteria for good work and how they show the student's learning. It is important to be able to tell students *exactly* what is going well and what has gone wrong in their assignments, but this needs to be done in a way that lets them feel secure and helps them see the opportunity for improvement. For example, 'This is irrelevant' might be a true criticism, but the student wonders why the information is not important. A stronger critical response that the student could take forward would be 'Although interesting, including information about Wordsworth's life does not explain how he used figurative language.' This sort of comment points the writer to the cause of the problem (difficulty selecting relevant information because of engagement with or interest in the topic) and explains how it fails to fulfil the requirements of the set task. Similarly, praise comments like 'I enjoyed reading your paper' do little to help the student think about what they did to make the text enjoyable for the reader. Stronger comments would use specific examples to support the positive evaluation; for example, 'I enjoyed reading this paper much more than the first version of it because you worked on structuring information so that it now makes sense and guides me through the paper.' This comment uses comparison to previous performance to show learner development, as well as explaining how and why taking action has improved something specific in the text.

Tutors would do well to remember that criticism and praise are often intimately connected in feedback practices. Tutors therefore need to balance constructive criticism with the power of positive comments that, when used sparingly, encourage student 'uptake' for the changes and learning that tutors want to instil. They must also be aware of the fact that criticism and praise are evaluative comments that judge the quality of students' work and that show students what the tutor values. Faber (1995) suggests tutors should always strive to give criticism that doesn't wound and praise that does not demean.

Praise and criticism, however, are not the only types of comments tutors can use. The following list summarizes the many types of response tutors can include in their feedback repertoire:

Correcting – comments that 'fix' the 'problem' (show errors): '1960s, not 1960's'.

Commanding – comments that tell the writer what to do and what not to do: 'Don't use each paragraph as a summary of part of a source.'

Evaluating – comments that provide some type of assessment: 'This is only half right.'

Suggesting – comments that offer editorial advice: 'Should this be attached to the previous sentence?' 'I had some trouble following the argument. To improve this, try to introduce the topics you are going to discuss in your introduction for the reader to connect each point and understand the significance of each argument.'

Explaining – comments that provide an explanation of what is and is not working: 'Be careful about using subjective words such as "genius" – one person might see it that way, but another might disagree – so try to avoid using these kinds of "red-flag-to-a-bull" words in order to show academic objectivity.'

Criticizing – comments that give a negative evaluation (and usually offer no advice about how to improve): 'Wrong!' 'There were several grammatical and spelling errors that made it difficult for me to follow the paper's ideas.'

Praising – comments that describe the paper or parts of it positively or offer encouraging remarks: 'The writing was quite confident and poised, and once I started reading the introduction, I wanted to read even more. Therefore, the introduction is good because it sets the tone of the whole paper, making it very insightful and attention getting.'

Describing – comments that describe the rhetorical function of the text (what the text is doing): 'This paragraph seems out of place.'

Assigning – comments that assign tasks related to revision: 'Add an example here.' 'When you revisit this draft, consider amplifying (expanding on) the concept of infidelity.'

Reminding – comments that connect textual features to prior learning (class discussions, handouts, conferences): 'The essay by Tom Smith we looked at in class would be a good model for you to follow here.'

Emoting – comments that imply a sense of shared humanity or identification with the writer: 'I agree with you here.' 'I never thought of it this way – interesting insight.'

Questioning – comments that ask 'real' questions: 'How does this idea connect with your thesis?' 'What are the consequences of this way of thinking?'

Alerting – symbols or words that indicate points made and/or mechanical errors: ticks, underlining, 'awk' and 'S/V agree'. (Be aware, however, that use of alerting should be used sparingly, if at all, since students do not always understand what is meant by these types of symbolically coded messages.)

Focusing – comments that address the text's adherence to a central point and/or answering the set question: 'You seem to drift from the central point on page 2 when talking about feudal law.' 'You have made a good attempt at conveying your understanding of the text and have considered how the techniques that the writers have employed have been successful.'

Last words?

There are numerous ways you can develop and hone your response style and practices. Learn by looking at what colleagues write on student scripts during the moderation process and study samples of effective tutors' comments. Read about principles of response and try to put them into practice. Identify favourite feedback strategies and try to create a broader repertoire of comments, and place these strategies in relation to students' learning needs and styles. Reflect on feedback practices and goals after every feedback situation to see if they are working.

Activity: 'Last words' – what have you learned about your response style?

Write a two-minute reflection on what you discovered about your feedback practices through engaging with the reflective activities. If you have trouble getting started, try writing a list of what you learned or any changes you'd like to make. At the end of two minutes, read what you've written and then draft an action plan for improving your feedback to students. Revisit this reflection from time to time, especially before and after you write comments on another set of student papers.

Students will generally welcome a detailed response to what they have written, as suggested by the NUS Charter on Feedback found in Chapter 5 (see pages 132–5). If they have gone to the trouble of producing 1500 words of close argument, they will rightly feel that they are entitled to more than just a few approving ticks in the margin and a percentage grade on the final page. But it is also possible for tutors to put too much comment on an essay. Striking the right balance is a matter of considerable experience, sensitivity and fine judgement. And, when in doubt about the quantity and quality of your feedback comments, ask your students about their preferences.

Recommended follow-up reading

Straub, R. (2000) *The Practice of Response: Strategies for Commenting on Student Writing.* Cresskill, NJ: Hampton Press.

4

'The Biggs picture'
Constructively aligned feedback

This chapter explores the way constructive alignment is the interplay between criteria and feedback and how criterion-referenced rubrics can articulate this interplay and communicate learning outcomes to students so that they can begin to take responsibility for their own learning. Please note that much of the discussion here will focus on feedback related to task-related performances rather than on writing to learn and understand. While we believe that the latter is extremely important for students' intellectual and personal development, we've chosen to limit our discussion to task performance because Biggs and others advocate aligning feedback with learning outcomes and, much to our chagrin, 'writing to learn' is too rarely included as an assignment (or module or course) learning outcome.

Aligning feedback with learning outcomes • Criterion-referenced rubrics and proformas • Sharing criterion-referenced rubrics as a way to feed back and forward • Final thoughts on feedback from a tutor perspective • Recommended follow-up reading

The term constructive alignment was coined by John Biggs (1999: 11), who explains it thus: 'The fundamental principle of constructive alignment is that a good teaching system aligns teaching method and assessment to the learning activities stated in the objectives so that all aspects of this system are in accord in supporting appropriate student learning.' Constructive alignment, then, rests on a view of teaching as supporting learning. What is important is not so much what tutors do as what students do. This implies a need for clarity about what it means for students to 'understand' and the kinds of teaching and learning activities required to reach those kinds of understandings.

Rust (2002: 148) summarizes Biggs's concept of constructive alignment into a three-staged model:

1 Identify clear learning outcomes.
2 Design appropriate assessment tasks that will directly assess whether each of the learning outcomes has been met.
3 Design appropriate learning opportunities for the students to get them to a point where they can successfully undertake the assessment tasks.

The main premise behind constructive alignment is the alignment of teaching and learning activities and the assessment modes with the learning outcomes. Tutors should therefore ask themselves, 'What should the students be able to do on completion of the course, the module, the learning unit?' Everything tutors do is then geared towards enabling students to achieve these learning outcomes and testing that the students have grasped the learning goals. In short, everything tutors do in a constructively aligned learning environment is aimed at supporting learning and ensuring that student performance becomes the focus of teaching and learning.

Since feedback is given in response to student performance, and student performance is an attempt to show mastery of a learning outcome or goal, clarity of the learning goal is where the feedback package begins. Tutors must be clear about their content area and mastery objectives, and they need to clearly communicate the desired learning outcome to students through instruction.

Aligning feedback with learning outcomes

Research has shown that effective feedback is an integral part of an instructional dialogue between the tutor and student (or between students, or between the student and him/herself). Black and Wiliam (1998a) identify three essential elements of what they term enhanced feedback: recognition of the desired goal; evidence about present position; and some understanding of a way to close the gap between the two. The starting point for tutor feedback, then, is the learning outcome. Aligning feedback with learning outcomes means giving feedback in reference to specific types of goals so that students know if they are on the right track and to what extent they have reached their goals through the feedback the tutor gives them.

Tutors need to have a clear idea of what they want students to be able to do at the end of a module or unit of study, and to communicate these intended learning outcomes to students so they can at least share in the responsibility of achieving them. Students, however, will inevitably tend to look at the assessment and structure their learning to optimize their assessment performance – their process will work towards the product rather than towards learning. As a result, students frequently have different understandings and approaches to learning goals. Hounsell (1997), for example, has shown that tutors and students often have quite different conceptions about the goals and criteria for essays and that poor essay performance is correlated with the degree of mismatch. Similarly, Norton (1990) has demonstrated that when students were asked to rank specific assessment criteria for an essay task, they produced quite different rankings from those of their tutors, emphasizing content above critical thinking and argument. Weak and incorrect conceptions of goals both influence how students perform on assessments and influence the way they value and use feedback information. If students do not share (at least in part) the tutor's conceptions of assessment goals (and their attendant criteria and standards) then the feedback information they receive is unlikely to 'connect' (Hounsell 1997). When this happens, it becomes difficult for students to evaluate discrepancies between required and actual performance. Feedback aligned with learning outcomes thus not only helps guide students towards academic goals but, over time, it also has a role in helping clarify what these goals are (Sadler 1989).

One strategy for ensuring students work towards mastery of learning outcomes and more self-regulated learning is through criterion-referenced assessments and feedback. Biggs (2003) has argued that for students to be engaged in a deeper process of learning, processes related to learning objectives and assessment must be aligned, and that such alignment should also favour criterion-referenced assessment rather than norm-referenced assessment. Criterion-referenced assessment and feedback attempt to uncover the strengths and weakness of a student in terms of what he or she knows or doesn't know, understands or doesn't understand, or can do or cannot do, as measured against a benchmark or standard.

Providing students with written documents containing statements that describe assessment criteria and/or the standards that define different levels of achievement helps clarify task-related goals/criteria/standards. However, numerous studies have shown that it is difficult to make assessment criteria and standards explicit through written documentation or through verbal descriptions in class (Rust et al. 2003). Most criteria for academic tasks are multidimensional and thus extremely complex (Sadler 1989). Additionally, criteria are difficult to articulate because they are often 'tacit' and in the mind of the teacher. As Yorke (2003: 480) notes: 'Statements of expected standards, curriculum objectives or learning outcomes are generally insufficient to convey the richness of meaning that is wrapped up in them.' Additionally, conceptions of criteria can vary between individual tutors, within disciplines and across different areas of study.

Despite the problems associated with making assessment criteria explicit and attempting to articulate the tacit, Sadler (1989: 3) contends that 'We need to let students into the secret, allowing them to become insiders of the assessment process. We need to make provision for them to become members of the guild of people who can make consistently sound judgments and know why those judgments are justifiable.' Tutors should therefore attempt to make sure that the assessment very obviously does test the learning outcomes so that students, by being strategic optimizers of their assessment performance, will actually be working towards achieving the intended learning outcomes. In other words, the learning outcomes and the assessment are aligned and therefore the assessment criteria should differ from the learning outcomes only in so far as that they might provide more details about levels of performance. If tutors tell students that they want them to achieve certain learning outcomes and then assess them against mismatched criteria, students will feel cheated and become strategic surface learners. Aligning feedback to learning outcomes criteria is ultimately a matter of fairness, transparency and honesty – of 'letting them into the secret' – which establishes the trust needed for students to confidently manage their own learning. Nicol and Macfarlane-Dick (2006b) suggest that certain strategies can prove effective in clarifying criteria, standards and goals, which include providing better definitions of requirements using carefully constructed criteria sheets and performance level definitions and making sure that feedback is provided in relation to pre-defined criteria but paying particular attention to the number of criteria.

Criterion-referenced rubrics and proformas

Numerous experts (e.g. Andrade 2001; Goodrich 1997; Brewer 1996; Marzano et al. 1993) believe that criterion-referenced rubrics improve students' end products and therefore increase learning. Andrade (2000) argues that criterion-referenced rubrics have the capacity to teach as well as evaluate student performance and as such are 'instructional'. Instructional rubrics are usually one- or two-page documents that can vary in format, but all share two common features: a list of criteria ('what counts') in a particular task or assignment; and gradations of quality for each criterion. Thus, when tutors evaluate assignments, they know implicitly what makes a good final product and why. When students receive rubrics beforehand, they understand how they will be evaluated and can prepare accordingly. Developing a rubric and making it available as a tool for students' use provides the scaffolding necessary to improve the quality of their work and increase their knowledge. Thus, rubrics quickly make sense to both tutors and students because they are clear, concise and digestible.

Rubrics are useful in assessment to inform learning since they contain qualitative descriptions of performance criteria, serving a valuable purpose for formative evaluation (Tierney and Simon 2004). Rubrics offer several other advantages: They do the following:

- improve student performance by clearly showing the student how their work will be evaluated and what is expected;
- help students become better judges of the quality of their own work;
- allow assessment to be more objective and consistent;
- force the tutor to clarify his/her criteria in specific terms;
- reduce the amount of time tutors spend evaluating student work;
- promote student awareness about the criteria to use in assessing peer performance;
- provide useful feedback to the tutor regarding the effectiveness of the instruction;
- provide students with more informative feedback about their strengths and areas in need of improvement;
- accommodate heterogeneous classes by offering a range of quality levels;
- are easy to use and easy to explain.

Well-designed rubrics clearly describe teachers' expectations and provide indicators of quality to be used by the students and the instructor. There are four basic types of instructional rubrics: generic, task-specific, holistic and analytic.

Generic rubrics are tools used to apply general criteria to a variety of student work, be it a product (things they make/write) or a performance (things they do), as long as each addresses the same objective or objectives. For example, a rubric that differentiates levels of accomplishment in portraying character, action, and environment in a dramatic presentation could also be used to score a solo performance, a group improvisation, or any number of other performance events. An example of a generic instructional rubric is provided in Table 4.1.

Activity-specific rubrics are the tools most often used for constructed response items that require a response based on a specific situation, assignment or stimulus. Similar to a generic rubric, an activity-specific rubric consists of brief descriptions of the characteristics of responses at each performance level. Activity-specific rubrics differ from generic rubrics in that descriptors only apply to one particular assessment activity, which may require a specific stimulus and specific response cues that include a specific number of response parts (e.g. elements of dance) and/or a specific content reference (e.g. Cubism). A generic rubric, for example, would include a descriptor such as 'an accurate and thorough explanation of how an artefact represents the culture in which it was produced', while an activity-specific rubric would say 'an accurate and thorough explanation of ways the tribal mask represents African culture'. Sometimes, changing only a few words or phrases can make a rubric activity-specific rather than generic. Conversely, changing those words or phrases to more comprehensive language allows them to be used with a limitless variety of assessment activities, as long as they address the same objectives. An example of a task-specific rubric is provided in Table 4.2.

Table 4.1 Generic rubric for first year students

A = outstanding performance	B = above average – very good	C = average – good	D = satisfactory performance	E = fail
Fully identifies a range of appropriate ideas, concepts and principles raised by the assignment.	Identifies some ideas, concepts and principles raised by the assignment.	Identifies most of the ideas, concepts and principles raised by the assignment.	Limited ability to identify ideas, concepts and principles raised by the assignment.	Very limited ability to identify appropriate ideas, concepts and principles raised by the assignment.
Excellent ability to apply ideas, concepts and principles covered in the module.	Good application of ideas, concepts and principles covered in the module.	Some application of ideas and knowledge covered in the module.	Limited application of ideas, concepts and knowledge covered in the module.	Very little application of ideas and knowledge covered in the module.
Is structured very effectively.	Is structured effectively.	Could have been structured more effectively.	Some problems with structuring the assignment.	Structure of assignment very confused.
Utilizes a wide range of material from independent sources to support and substantiate assignment remit.	Utilizes a good range of material from independent sources to support and substantiate own ideas/opinions.	Utilizes some material from independent sources to support assignment remit. Contained occasional sweeping or unjustified statements.	Does not utilize much appropriate material from independent sources to support assignment remit. Is sometimes descriptive. Some irrelevant material included. Contained many sweeping or unjustified statements.	Utilizes very little appropriate material from independent sources to support assignment remit. Is often descriptive. Irrelevant material included. Contained mainly sweeping or unjustified statements.
Uses accurate appropriate citation. Quotes and paraphrased materials are incorporated very effectively into the text.	Generally uses accurate and appropriate citation. Quotes and paraphrased materials are incorporated effectively into the text.	Some errors in accuracy and appropriateness of citation. Quotes and paraphrasing were sometimes incorporated effectively into the text.	Limited accuracy and appropriateness of citations. Quotes and paraphrasing were often not incorporated effectively into the text.	Lack of reference list and inaccurate and largely inappropriate use of citations. Quotes and paraphrasing were rarely incorporated effectively into the text.
The writing is clear and fluent with very occasional, minor errors in grammar, spelling or punctuation.	The writing is clear and fluent. The grammar, spelling and punctuation is mostly accurate.	The writing is easy to understand but there were systematic errors in grammar, spelling and punctuation.	The writing is not always easy to understand. There were many errors in grammar, spelling and punctuation.	The writing was frequently not easy to follow. There were many errors of spelling, grammar and function hindered understanding.

Source: Reproduced with permission from Amanda French, University of Wolverhampton, School of Education, 2009

Table 4.2 Example of task-specific rubric for ESL lesson, 'Visit to London monuments'

	A	B	C	D
Narration	A well-organized and connected story; includes details or elaboration about all photos in the task.	Story is mostly organized and connected; includes some details or elaboration about most photos in the task.	Story is a series of loosely connected events; includes few details or elaboration about photos in the task.	Story is an unconnected list of events; includes no details or elaboration about photos in the task.
Use of past tense	Uses past tense at all appropriate times; use is accurate.	Uses past tense frequently; use is mostly accurate.	Uses other tenses sometimes where past is appropriate; use is accurate some of the time.	Makes few attempts to use past tense; use is frequently inaccurate.
Cultural knowledge	Demonstrates extensive and correct knowledge of current and historical significance of all monuments.	Demonstrates adequate and correct knowledge of current and historical significance of most monuments.	Demonstrates partial and usually correct knowledge of current and historical significance of some monuments.	Demonstrates minimal or no knowledge of current and historical significance of monuments.

In addition to using generic and activity-specific rubrics, tutors can also use holistic and analytic rubrics to provide different types of feedback. Holistic rubrics provide a general feedback for the total product or process. Analytic rubrics feed back on individual components of the product or process and sum these scores to determine the total score. In choosing between them, it is useful to consider their relative strengths and weaknesses in relation to the purpose of assessment and the nature of the attributes that are being assessed, remembering that in professional education, the most important outcomes are likely to be holistic. Table 4.3 provides an overview of analytic and holistic rubrics.

Table 4.3 Analytic and holistic rubrics

	Analytic rubric	Holistic rubric
Features	• Performance assessed along separate dimensions and grade determined by adding scores of the various parts. • Criterion written for each dimension at each level (e.g. four criteria need to be written for a rubric that consists of two dimensions and two levels (2×2)). • Different weighting may be allocated to each dimension to account for their relative importance.	• No distinctions between dimensions and judgement made on the overall performance. • Only qualities associated with each level of performance specified.
When to use	• When the performance can be meaningfully broken down into distinct parts. • To provide formative feedback on specific dimension.	• When overall evaluation is needed. • When the intended outcome means more than the sum of its constituent parts.
Limitations	• Breaking down a performance into separate dimensions may risk missing the performance's overall integrity.	• A common perception is that a holistic assessment is too 'subjective' (however, clearly stated criteria should meet this limitation).

Source: Adapted from Assessment Resource Centre (2005)

Mertler (2001) provides the following process for designing rubrics:

1 Match learning objectives, instruction and the rubric's categories.
2 Identify specific observable attributes demonstrating mastery or understanding.
3 Define characteristics to describe the attributes.
4 Write narrative descriptions
   • Holistic: write complete descriptions for the highest and lowest level of performance using each attribute in each description (high level with all attributes and low level with all attributes).

- Analytic: write complete descriptions for the highest and lowest level of performance for each attribute (each individual attribute will have a high and a low level).
5 Describe intermediate levels of performance.
6 Collect student work samples illustrating each level.
7 Revise the rubric as necessary.

Tierney and Simon (2004) suggest that many rubrics can end up flawed due to a lack of consistency across the performance criteria descriptors. Performance criteria reflect the 'dimensions of the performance or product that is being taught and assessed' (p. 5). These authors recommend that the performance criteria should remain consistent from level to level. Put simply, the attributes listed in each criterion should be the same across all levels of quality. Another common mistake that causes a lack of consistency across the criteria is the use of excessively negative language to describe categories on the lower end of the quality continuum and excessively positive descriptors for the opposite end of the continuum.

Activity: Designing your own criterion-referenced feedback rubric

1 Using the template provided in Table 4.4, create a learning rubric that both fits your teaching/feedback style and is pitched at the appropriate level for students in one of your modules.

Table 4.4 Rubric template (Describe the task or performance this rubric is designed to evaluate.)

Describe gradation→	'Beginning' 1	'Developing' 2	'Accomplished' 3	'Exemplary' 4	Score
State objective or performance	Description of identifiable performance characteristics reflecting lowest level of performance. ↓	Description of identifiable performance characteristics reflecting development and movement towards mastery of performance. ↓	Description of identifiable performance characteristics reflecting mastery of performance. ↓	Description of identifiable performance character-istics reflecting the highest level of performance. ↓	
State objective or performance					
State objective or performance					

2 Now select an assessment task from the same module and identify the learning outcomes to be assessed. What criteria would you use to determine whether students have successfully met those outcomes? How would you describe them for your students? What levels of performance can be anticipated and expected?

3 Using both the above, create an instructional rubric that clarifies learning outcomes and assessment criteria, and establishes the graduations of quality for each criterion.

Perhaps the most common challenge to designing instructional rubrics that provide feedback and feedforward for students is avoiding unclear language. If a rubric is to teach as well as evaluate, all terms used must be defined for students – regardless of how difficult that may be. Similarly, avoiding unnecessarily negative language is crucial to engaging students with the rubric. For example, students need to know exactly what they did wrong and how they can do better next time, not just that the opening to their presentation or essay was 'boring'.

Articulating gradations of quality can also be a challenge. It is helpful for tutors to spend a good deal of time thinking about criteria and how best to chunk them before going on to define the levels of quality. According to Andrade (2001: 3), well-wrought rubrics should: be written in language students can understand; define and describe the quality of work; refer to common weaknesses in students' work and indicate how such weaknesses can be avoided; and guide revision or future performance. She offers the following as useful steps to designing rubrics that 'boost the[ir] learning leverage' and includes students in the process:

1 *Look at models:* Show students examples of good and not-so-good work. Identify the characteristics that make the good ones good and the bad ones bad.
2 *List criteria:* Use the discussion of models to begin a list of what counts in quality work.
3 *Articulate gradations of quality:* Describe the best and worst levels of quality, then fill in the middle levels based on your knowledge of common problems and the discussion of not-so-good work.
4 *Practise on models:* Have students use the rubrics to evaluate the models you gave them in Step 1.
5 *Use self- and peer-assessment:* Give students their task. As they work, stop them occasionally and give opportunities for engaging in peer review and self-assessment.
6 *Revise:* Always give students time to revise their work based on the feedback they get in Step 5.
7 *Use teacher assessment:* Use the same rubric students used to assess their work yourself.

Designing instruction rubrics following the above steps recognizes that the criteria should be clear, should be explicit and should be communicated to students, which is a major feature of the literature on feedback for learning. Additionally, providing students with opportunities to discuss, define and agree on criteria for their assessed work – perhaps even writing them with negotiation – is considered important to fostering self-regulated learning. In particular, the literature on self- and peer assessment stresses that students perceive that they have more direct involvement with the whole assessment process (Boud and Falchikov 1989; Stefani 1998), which in turn encourages them to become more aware of and use the assessment criteria to direct their learning.

Sharing criterion-referenced rubrics as a way to feed back and forward

Feedback is more effective if it focuses on the learning intention of the task and is given regularly while still relevant. However, providing frequent feedback on student assignments can be particularly difficult in large modules. More importantly, when the tutor is the sole provider of feedback, it can reinforce the tutor's authority as grade-giver and create a culture of tutor dependency (Dheram 1995). It is therefore important to get students engaged in the assessment and learning activities and to make them aware that their involvement in them is crucial to improving their learning. When students learn how to respond to and evaluate their own and their peers' work, tutors can shift attention to other responsibilities and students become more self-regulated learners.

According to Dunlap and Grabinger (cited in Dunlap 2005: 20), 'the process of reviewing someone else's work can help learners reflect on and articulate their own views and ideas, ultimately improving their own work'. Additionally, responding to others' texts also gives students an insight into the assignment or task's standard of performance. This is especially the case when students are encouraged to use criterion-referenced rubrics that focus on achieving the intended learning outcomes. By using such rubrics, students begin to internalize the criteria or standards for high-quality work and the descriptions of progressive levels of performance serve as feedback that offers guidance about what they need to do to improve their performance.

Peer review and self-assessment

By asking students to read and evaluate a fellow student's work, peer review activities cast students in the role of tutors. Such activities require reviewers to apply the knowledge and experience they have gained in class and in producing their own work. These activities also engage students in the cognitive process of elaboration by having them relate their criticisms and advice to someone else, an activity demonstrated in the literature to improve the learning of its practitioners. The student whose work is critiqued receives the benefit of comments and recommendations from multiple tutors. In addition to these cognitive benefits, appropriately structured peer review activities that include a clearly worded and explained assessment rubric can help students learn professional/academic standards and practices and afford opportunities to apply them in realistic settings. Peer review can also be effective because students can clarify their own ideas and understanding of both the learning intention and the assessment criteria while reading and responding to other students' work.

Asking students to look at examples of other students' work that does and does not meet the instructional rubric's criteria can help them to understand what was required from a task and to assess the next steps they might need to take. Looking at different responses to a particular task can also help students understand the different approaches they could have taken. Topping's (1998) review of the literature on peer review, for example, shows that it can have positive formative effects on student achievement and attitudes. Peer review must be managed carefully, though. Students are unlikely to spontaneously produce brilliant responses to their peers' work even when they have been involved in defining the criteria, so the usefulness of peer review depends upon the instructions and guidance tutors give students. In particular, it must be made clear to the students that using the rubric is not for the purpose of ranking or grading because if students compare themselves with others rather than their own previous attainment, those performing better than their peers will not be challenged and those performing worse will be demotivated.

For peer review to work effectively, then, the learning environment in the classroom must be supportive. Students must feel comfortable and trust one another in order to provide honest and constructive feedback. One effective way to promote this type of environment is to use group work and peer review frequently. To help students develop trust, form them into small groups early in the semester and have them work in the same groups throughout the term. Give them opportunities to practise using the rubrics on similar types of assignments that were written by students they do not know. This allows them to become more comfortable with each other, with the criteria and leads to better peer feedback.

Like peer review, self-assessment is an important tool for providing feedback. Once students understand how to use the rubrics to assess their current knowledge and the gaps in it, they will have a clearer idea of how they can help themselves progress. Tutors and students can then set targets relating to specific criteria included on the rubric so that students will be able to guide their own learning, with the tutor providing help where necessary or appropriate. Tutors need to remember, though, that students do not learn to monitor or assess their learning on their own. They need to be taught strategies for self-monitoring and self-assessment. One way to help students become more comfortable and confident with self-assessment (and peer review) is for the tutor to model the technique by using a criterion-referenced rubric. Students can then try the technique themselves and discuss how well the technique worked and what to do differently next time. One example of this sort of rubric is provided in Table 4.5, while other rubrics and proformas intended to help students prepare to use feedback in peer review and for personal develop planning are provided in Chapter 8.

Table 4.5 Self-assessment rubric

	Needs considerable work (E/F)	Needs more work (D)	Adequate (C)	Good (B)	Very good (A)
1 Content					
2 Structure					
3 Conventions					
4 Sources					
5 Style					

If I had more time, how would I improve this essay and my future essays?
1
2
3
4
5

Moderator Comments:
1
2
3
4
5

Complete this form to the best of your ability, using the assessment descriptors provided. Your module tutor will act as moderator and make comments in response to your self-assessment. You should also include specific comments for improvement on this assignment and for future ones.

It is important to point out that peer review and self-assessment using criterion-referenced rubrics are processes which are vital to whatever assessment is used (Cooper 2000). In the context of changing patterns of student assessment in higher education, clarity about the nature and scope of assessment criteria aligned with learning outcomes and activities is important. Instructional rubrics provide tutors and students with important information that makes clear what the purpose and criteria for assessment are.

And when used as part of peer review and self-assessment, constructively aligned instructional rubrics show students where they have been, where they are now, and where they need to be. They also help students learn how to monitor their own learning, develop the ability to judge and evaluate their own and their peers' work, as well as think about what to do next. When tutors involve students in the feedback and assessment processes, they shift some of the responsibility for documenting and justifying learning back to the students.

Final thoughts on feedback from a tutor perspective

Table 4.6 provides an overview of the types of learning rubrics you can use. Remember to consider how the rubric will both provide your students with information about their performance and how it can be aligned to the learning outcomes being assessed. Consider ways you can encourage and engage students in creating outcome-aligned assessment criteria, and afford them opportunities to use perhaps more than one type of rubric in their exchanges with peers.

Table 4.6 Types and uses of rubrics

Types	Purpose/distinction	Focal use
Holistic	Provide a single score based on an overall impression of learner achievement on a task	To provide overall evaluation guidelines that clarify how grades relate to performance/achievement, such as in course grades
Analytic	Provide specific feedback along several dimensions	To break assignments or scores down into separate components for grading (description, analysis, grammar, references, etc.)
Generic	Contain criteria that are general across tasks	Designed to provide general guidance as to expectations, such as for grading of written assignments
Task-specific	Are unique to a task/assignment	Designed to provide detailed guidance regarding a specific assignment or task

Source: Adapted from Schreyer Institute for Teaching Excellence (2007)

Feedback is an important part of teaching and learning, and one of the ways students learn and progress best is by receiving feedback on their performance. While feedback can be both formal and informal, evidence suggests that it fulfils a variety of purposes, which tutors would do well to bear in mind:

- Explains what students have done: *describes, clarifies, informs*
- Identifies strengths and weaknesses: *diagnoses, differentiates, remediates*
- Helps students to move forward: *motivates, liberates, empowers*
- Indicates a student's position/standing: *predicts, qualifies, licenses*
- Assists with module/course/programme evaluation: *maintains standards, monitors*

Recommended follow-up reading

Race, P., Brown, S. and Smith, B. (2005) *500 Tips on Assessment*, 2nd edn. Abingdon: Routledge.

Part II

The reception of feedback by students

'Now I've got the feedback, what do I do with it?' This question from a first year student highlights the issue raised by Gibbs (2006: 26): 'The crucial variable appears not to be the quality of feedback but the quality of student engagement with that feedback.' This text holds that both aspects of quality are important, but agrees with Gibbs that major issues arise in student engagement, or rather lack of engagement, with tutor feedback.

This section of the book explores issues concerning the reception of tutor feedback by students. If you are progressing through the book you may have developed your feedback techniques and feel that you are providing students with good written feedback on their work. However, the 'gift' you provide in your feedback will not be revealed until the student peels off the wrapping and engages with your comments (Askew and Lodge 2000). Students can seem reluctant to take the step of reading feedback on their work and thus miss out on the valuable advice that we, as experts in learning in our subjects, provide in our written comments. Thus, it is necessary to explore reasons why students are not making more use of our feedback, and then to consider how we can address these obstacles in our feedback policies.

This section begins with a consideration of student perspectives on tutor feedback, drawing on research and official Student Union documents, to set out how feedback looks to those on the receiving end. Sharing this perspective will enable us to consider the implications for our practice, and explore ways to address the problems identified by students.

The heart of this section is an exploration of ways to help students get more out of our feedback. The first step is an exploration of ways to prepare students for feedback; this is essentially cognitive preparation to enable students to develop an understanding of the place tutor feedback can play in their learning journey. This new cognitive perspective needs to be turned into concrete actions by students and the last two chapters present a range of strategies for using feedback more effectively. These chapters work outwards from subject tutor input in unpacking feedback, to a consideration of the range of supports that are available to help students address the issues raised in tutor feedback.

This exploration links to the ASK approach to learning, developed by Burke and Pieterick to underpin their work, as part of Burke's National Teacher Fellowship project and Pieterick's work within the Centre for Excellence in Teaching and Learning: Critical Interventions for Enhanced Learning (CIEL). This approach seeks to bring a change in attitudes (A) to study to prevent early closure, which is supported by introducing students to a range of strategies (S) for learning, leading to knowledge (K), both cognitive and practical, to guide student learning. Chapter 7 explores the cognitive aspects of this approach while Chapter 8 explores practical strategies for students to use in unpacking and acting on tutor feedback. The ASK approach encourages students to develop their attitude to tutor comments, so that they are seen to go beyond feedback on past work to feedforward into future learning. With regard to knowledge, students gain the cognitive perspective that feedback is integral to their learning as it provides evidence of their achievement and indicates areas for development.

The underpinning ASK approach arms students with a cognitive foundation and a range of practical strategies to enable them to get more out of tutor feedback. The aim is to keep the communication channels between student and tutor open so that the feedback continues to *talk with* students and inform their future learning.

5

Feedback from a student perspective

This chapter sets the scene for the student section by setting out research on student views on feedback. This foundation makes it possible to see gaps between tutor and student views on feedback. Most importantly this chapter reminds us of the emotional challenge presented by external judgements for students on their work.

The gap between tutor and student perceptions on feedback • Research on student views: what do students think about feedback? • What students want • Psychological impact of feedback: emotional aspect • The Feedback Amnesty (A National Student Charter on Feedback, UK) • Recommended follow-up reading

'Unconsolidated argument! What on earth does that mean?' These words from a student to a friend as she looked at the feedback on her essay introduce the student theme. How often do such conversations take place between students when they get work back from tutors. Tutors may be familiar with academic terms, but if students do not share these meanings then the feedback communication breaks down. Tutors may not remember what it was like to be a learner receiving feedback on their work, as Falchikov (1995: 157) reminds: 'There is a great deal that we as teachers can learn from students about the level and quality of feedback they find most useful.' On a basic level this may be a reminder of a practical issue that is easy to put right, such as avoiding writing comments in red ink or using red font as Haines (2004: 20) reports: 'There is anecdotal evidence that students respond to comments or grades written in red with higher anxiety and hostility than to comments in other colours.' More importantly and concerning the content of feedback, Haines informs that listening to student views on feedback can guide us as to how students are likely to 'receive and interpret our comments'.

This chapter aims to explore such student perspectives, and these insights will enable us to remember the recipients of our feedback when we are marking. We need to consider what students want from us in our feedback on their work, building on the earlier section (see pp. 20–1) which sets out research from Straub on 'what students want'. Responding to such needs can help us provide feedback that facilitates student learning. In addition we need to listen to the ways students receive the feedback we provide, to ensure that at the point of receiving feedback students feel emotionally confident to unpack feedback, and have developed the skills to interpret and act on it.

The gap between tutor and student perceptions on feedback

Walker (2009: 76) raised the question 'why are tutors providing such a high proportion of comments that are unlikely to be usable?' MacLellan's (2001) research provides one answer to this question in the gap identified between tutor and student perceptions on the role of feedback within student learning. For example, she found that 43 per cent of tutors thought that feedback *frequently* 'is helpful in detail', whereas 73 per cent of students found that feedback is *sometimes* 'helpful in detail'. More telling was the perception from 63 per cent of tutors that feedback *frequently* 'prompts discussion with tutor', but who tutors had discussion with is questionable as 50 per cent of students found feedback *never* prompted discussion. This finding that 50 per cent of students did not discuss feedback with their tutor, suggests limited discussion between tutors and students about feedback. Thus, many tutors may be unaware of such negative student views about the benefit of feedback for their learning.

MacLellan's research suggests that tutors work from the assumption that the feedback they provide on student work is successful in aiding student learning. However, her summary of this research revealed that many students do not find tutor feedback helpful in detail, that feedback does not prompt discussion with tutors, nor does feedback help students understand the assessment process or improve their learning. These negative perceptions of feedback have also been found in the National Student Satisfaction Survey (UK) and research studies from the Americas and the Far East (Sprinkle 2004; Carless 2006).

Returning to Walker's question about comment usability, the answer to why tutors spend so much time producing unusable feedback appears to be found in minimal monitoring by tutors of student reception and use of feedback. I mark electronically and keep a copy of my comments and often note that I am making the same comment to the same student year after year. However, I only note this retrospectively as I mark anonymously and thus do not consider who the student is at the point of marking. It is only at a later stage when I meet with individual students that discussion may uncover the fact that similar comments have been made in the past. Perhaps this fact that we write similar things to the same students time after time indicates that the feedback is not working for students; they either do not understand it or they do not know what to do with it.

Do you know how students use your comments? What feedback would you expect students to give you on your feedback on their essays?

Activity: Dare you ask? Finding out what students think about your feedback

Which of the following provides you with information about student views on your feedback?

- Individual student comments during feedback tutorials where you can see which comments they have understood and which need further explanation
- Module evaluation forms which provide student views on written feedback
- Reports from student representatives
- Evidence that students have acted on comments in future pieces of work
- Other

Research on student views: what do students think about feedback?

Students appear to enter higher education with a positive view about feedback. In a survey of 350 students at induction in 2006 (Burke 2009a), 69 per cent of students reported that feedback from teachers had helped their learning in the past. Many students gave examples of how feedback helped their learning, for example: 'Guidance given by tutors who marked essays, explained why certain things were said which enabled me to interpret what was meant and how to provide changes necessary.' However, such a positive view of feedback is not common in the end-of-year results of the UK National Student Survey. Year on year students nationally express dissatisfaction with the form and content of tutor feedback on their work.

The overall response from various studies is that students are confused, frustrated and dissatisfied with the feedback they receive on their work. Walker's (2009) study itemized areas of dissatisfaction: it is too brief, feedback is often provided by way of terms that students do not understand, and feedback can make assumptions about the amount of work students have done. Lillis and Turner (2001) found that feedback could raise more questions for students than it answered if students do not understand the terms used by tutors in their feedback. Chanock (2000) provided a concrete example of this problem in the fact that only half of students surveyed (51 per cent) understood what the term 'analysis' meant in their feedback.

We probably all have our own key words that we use time and again in feedback, for example, Burke owns up to using 'substantiate' and 'status of material' while Pieterick uses 'underdeveloped analysis' and 'hasty generalization'. We assume that students will interpret these sorts of comments in light of the preparation for academic work provided in core modules and key subject documentation. But it may well be the case that other tutors will have their own key phrases for when they want students to back up points with evidence (substantiate), or when tutors are not clear if the words used are the student's own words or from another source (status of material).

Activity: Can't read it, don't understand it! Problems students report concerning feedback

---

Arrange these comments from students on feedback into rows, putting the statements you think students are most likely to make at the top and the ones they are least likely to make at the bottom.

It takes so long to get feedback, that I can't remember doing the work.	I can't read the comments!	Comments make judgements about my attitude or efforts that are not true.
There is so much feedback that I can't make sense of it.	It only says good, but does not say why it is good.	Comments are brief and vague.
I can't see a connection between the comments and the grade.	The comments do not take me anywhere.	Often feedback is confusing and offers conflicting advice.

These actual responses from students are a good place to start in considering student perceptions of problems they encounter with tutor feedback. If these responses are turned round then we can start to identify what students actually want from feedback. We see that students want a quick response, they want to be able to read the feedback, they want it to relate to marking criteria, and they want it to be consistent. They also want the feedback to indicate how they can move their learning on, whatever the level of achievement. This developmental aspect is supported by Walker's (2009: 75) findings:

> Two themes emerged strongly. One was that they wished to be told what they had got wrong, and why, and how to do better. It should be noted that the 'why' indicates a wish for an explanation. The other was that they would appreciate being given things to work on or watch out for in future assignments, or just receiving general suggestions for their future assignments.

What students want

Cottrell (2001) reported on a range of student frustrations with feedback, and suggested that students were unlikely to use feedback that was intrusive or demoralizing, or if it was too detailed and offered too many suggestions for improvement. Her list stressed the importance of alignment, as set out earlier by Biggs (1999: 79–80), that students should be able to understand feedback, they should be motivated by it and able to act on it.

The following points set out a student 'wish list' on feedback, drawn from student comments in my studies (Burke 2007a, 2009a).

The right amount of information

Students want enough feedback to let them know how successful their learning in the particular assignment had been for the feedback to guide their future learning. It might come as something of a surprise to conscientious tutors who provide very detailed feedback that students may struggle to interpret feedback if there is too much of it. We might expect students to express problems with very brief feedback, such as single word comments like 'unsatisfactory', as there is clearly nothing to inform students about their learning. But it seems strange that student learning may not benefit from detailed feedback. Bloxham and West (2007: 85) reported on a study with students in which one group received less feedback than the other. They hypothesized 'that less feedback helps the students to focus on one or two key areas'. There may also have been qualitative issues in this instance, as the feedback was fit for purpose in providing advice that was very specific and guided students through concrete actions for tasks.

However, if too much feedback can cause confusion, students also report dissatisfaction with feedback that lacks detail. They often find themselves unable to interpret squiggles made on their work, or to know what to make of words followed by a question or exclamation mark. Students state that they need clear information on their performance in relation to the set learning outcomes for the task; they need to know what they did right and which aspects need to be developed.

Accessibility

Students need to be able to access the feedback they receive on their work. On one level this relates to basic legibility: students need to be able to read handwritten comments. On a higher level, students need to be able to understand the comments made and the implications of the comments. Race et al. (2005: 105) recommend that students should 'not have to struggle to make sense of our feedback'; they should be able to gain necessary information from the first reading of our comments.

This means that the terms we use in feedback should be ones students are familiar with. This can be provided through cross-references to the terminology used for the assessment criteria so students know where they stand. Student learning will also be enhanced by codes or keys which help students interpret squiggles made on scripts. Many staff are experienced in publishing and may use publishing shorthand to identify corrections or changes required on the script. Prior preparation for students with terminology and codes before they receive feedback can help them make sense of our feedback.

Students also want comments written for them, to inform them about their learning. Sometimes comments seem to have been written for another audience, to provide a justification for the grade to internal moderators or external examiners. Such comments do not enable students to access information about their learning and how to develop it.

Consistency

Students want consistency in feedback; this means consistency both within and between assessments. Students express the need for alignment between marks and tutor comments. Student comments indicate the problems that occur when the feedback provided does not add up, for example, when the feedback comments are very positive but do not fit with a low grade, or conversely when the grade is high but the comments are negative.

Second, there is an issue about consistency between tutors and subjects. Students are frustrated and confused when they seem to get different feedback from different sources. One student reported on her experience: 'Some teachers gave useful advice, then you try and apply the new learnt skills on the next essay and you get a better grade but as soon as you have another teacher, that teacher might not agree and give you a worse grade' (Burke 2009b). This sets out the student perception that marking was not in relation to standard criteria but according to the individual whim of the tutor, thus making it necessary for students to consider each tutor's preferred style of presentation. This leads many students to regard feedback as a personal judgement on their work rather than an objective academic assessment. Regarding feedback as an idiosyncratic response by individual tutors minimizes the opportunity for feedback to be used for self-monitoring by students. If students receive negative feedback, they may put this down to the tutor not liking them, rather than use it as evidence for their development within the subject.

Prompt feedback

Falchikov (1995) noted the psychological requirement for feedback to be provided as close to the behaviour as possible. She built on Bruner's (1970) view that learning depends on 'knowledge of results, at a time when, and at a place where, the knowledge can be used for correction' (Falchikov 1995: 157). Student comments support this requirement; they want to know the results of their assignments while the learning activities are fresh.

They talk of needing to know how they have done before they move on to the next task, in order to be able to act on feedback advice. In modules where students have two pieces of assessment, they express the desire to receive feedback on the first task before they move on to the second. This is often a problem in modular courses when students have to get so far into the semester to produce the first piece of work, then a three-week period may elapse before they receive feedback. Thus, students may face hand-in dates that do not allow them the opportunity to receive feedback on the first assignment before they hand in the second assignment. Students express frustration when the feedback on the first assignment identified a problem in their work, which they have not been able to put right, and may have replicated in the second assignment. This frustration is exacerbated when the feedback on the second assignment makes the same negative comment on the point, which the student is now aware of, and this frustration is made even worse if the irritated tutor response questions why the student has not acted on advice given in the first assignment.

Constructive feedback, providing direction

Students did not find feedback helpful if the tutor comments were too vague, if the feedback focused on negatives, or if the feedback failed to provide guidance. All too often students reported that corrective feedback, which signalled grammatical mistakes or errors in fact, was problematic if they did not know how to put it right, as illustrated by this student comment: 'They showed me how to correct it but it didn't look to stop what was making me make the mistakes' (Burke 2009b).

Essentially students want feedback that aids their progress, whether they are at the top or bottom end of the learning scale. High fliers are frustrated by feedback that praises the level of achievement but does not indicate how the student could progress in future assignments. One student who received a high grade for her essay stated: 'Can you tell me what exactly is right and what I should do next time and if the essay was so good why didn't I get a higher grade? There must have been something that needs improvement' (Burke 2009b).

Generally students seemed to accept that feedback should be corrective, but only when feedback showed them how to improve. Students valued balanced comments, which not only showed the student where they had gone wrong but also showed how to put things right.

Non-judgemental feedback

Students report the feeling that tutors judge rather than assess their work. While there may only be a marginal semantic difference between the acts of judging and assessing, for students who are on the receiving end this difference can be important. One difference between an assessment and a judgement is located in the language used. Brown and Glover (2006: 83) drew on Rorty's (1989) recommendation to avoid 'final vocabulary' in feedback, as such 'value-laden, judgemental words [that] may inhibit further learning by damaging students' self-esteem'.

Generally, we understand that judgements are received and although there may be a formal process of appeal, they are not open to debate. Thus, for students to perceive tutors judging in their feedback is problematical as students are likely to stand passively in the receipt of such feedback. There is the additional issue of being judged and the implications when work is deemed to be below standard. Yorke (2002) reminded of the sense of humiliation that can accompany judgements about student's work, which can result in lack of confidence and withdrawal.

Haines (2004: 23) provided an insight into the way students receive critical feedback comments. For example, simplistic comments that advise the student to be 'more concise or specific' may not seem problematical from a tutor's point of view. However, from the student's, such comments fail to appreciate the decisions the student had to make in planning which content to include and the level of depth to pursue. Thus, Haines reports student outpourings such as 'I thought you wanted details?' or a response to more details required: '*You* be more specific. It's going to be way too long', the student response showing frustration that the tutor has underestimated the thinking that went into the assignment. Equally, the simplistic comment 'Try harder' fails to appreciate how hard the student has tried, as indicated by this response: 'Maybe I'm trying as hard as I can! I did try! This comment makes me feel really bad and I'm frustrated.'

Exemplars

Most of points raised so far have been changes that students require to rectify deficiencies in the feedback they receive. The area of exemplars is slightly different as it is an area of good practice that students have identified positively and they would like more model answers or examples of marked work to see the application of marking criteria.

Brown and Glover's (2006) study with Open University students reported that students identified feedback as useful if it helped them close the gap between current performance and future improved performance. One way this was done was through the provision of specimen answers, which explained why the answer was successful in addressing the set task. My current research on the use of hyperlinks and linked webfolios, Case Studies 6 and 7, follows the same line, and student responses to these initiatives are very positive. Students report that the inclusion of a hyperlink to materials that addressed the learning need identified in feedback, meant they were likely to follow up that feedback. In addition, the use of Webfolios, that provided exemplars on the tasks undertaken, helped them to 'see' what was required. These examples of marked work enabled students to stand back from their work and use the external standard to reflect on it in an objective manner.

Psychological impact of feedback: emotional aspect

Many of the comments from students reveal an emotional reaction to the feedback received on their work. This shows a student tendency to read feedback as a statement of praise or blame on them as individuals. While tutors present the assessment process as an objective academic exercise by which they assess student work according to rational criteria, many students interpret comments in an irrational way as a judgement on them personally.

Before we move on to consider how our students perceive our written feedback on their work, let us pause for a moment and consider our own experiences of negative feedback on our work. Perhaps going back to feedback we received as undergraduates is a step too far, so instead we will consider feedback we receive on our professional practice, be it peer observation of teaching or peer review of articles.

Activity: How does it feel? Receiving feedback on your work

'The title is a bit weak, long-winded and descriptive. A more direct title is suggested. The text used a plodding and subject-indeterminate passive form, and some awkward construction, such as, "The results identified . . . to be . . .". Sentences tend to be long and over-structured . . .'

'Overall I found the paper meritorious, but difficult to read . . . it would help the authors' case if they tightened up their writing style a bit, especially in the discussion, which is much too long' (Murray 2005: 195).

What would your initial reaction to these comments be?

Would you talk to anyone about the comments?

Would your views change over time?

Murray's section in *Writing for Academic Journals* (2005) on tutor experiences of others assessing their work is largely an account of ways to cope with negative feedback. I will own up to opening emails or letters from journal editors with a sense of trepidation. Sometimes negative words jump out of the page and take over your perception of the correspondence. It may be that a negative comment such as 'plodding style' generates such an emotional response that it prevents you from seeing that the overall response is positive and the recommendation is to publish the article.

Murray also noted that we are likely to question the authority of the person providing the feedback, and question the right they have to make such judgements. We often feel a sense of frustration when reviewers nitpick or miss the point we were trying to make, or when there is a suggestion to cover something that you decided to leave out. We can also feel a sense of outrage when there is a suggestion that 'you do not seem to know what you are writing about'. This emotional reaction to feedback can engender what Murray (2005: 196) terms a 'sense of personal grievance' towards a review that can 'inhibit revision and resubmission'.

Are our experiences as academics similar to the experiences of students? Some aspects are clearly different as we face a much greater loss of credibility in the face of negative feedback. But the emotional reaction may actually be worse for students. If we as experienced learners are hit for six by feedback, how much worse is it likely to be for our undergraduates? Widening participation means that many students are the first from their family to enter higher education, and may lack supportive family networks. Thus, they are not able to share their anxieties with their family, as they may feel their family will not understand, or they may not want to admit to self-doubt in the face of friends and family who do not value higher education, or who think that the individual is over-stepping the mark in going to university. (The next chapter explores ways to prepare students for feedback and central to such considerations is psychological scaffolding to provide students with the support they need to make sense of, cope with and act on tutor feedback.)

Activity: A balancing act – your balance between positive and negative comments

Take five marked essays and write out each positive and negative comment on them.
What is the balance between positive/negative? How do you think a student is likely to respond to this balance?

The Feedback Amnesty (A National Student Charter on Feedback, UK)

Since the early 2000s there has been increasing dialogue and joint action between student bodies and higher education institutions. The Feedback Amnesty is one example of such partnership, and provides an official student-led statement on the feedback students want on their work. This chapter concludes with the executive summary of the ten principles of feedback from the National Union of Students (NUS) Vice President, Aaron Porter.

Student responses in the National Student Survey consistently rated feedback on assessment lower than other aspects of their experience. This led to the National Union of Students (UK) to explore issues related to feedback in The *Great NUS Feedback Amnesty* in 2008 (see Wicklow 2009). Working from the results of the 2008 National Student Survey (NSS), the NUS initiated the feedback campaign due to 'pervasive and continuous' problems with feedback. The aim was to address 'poor mechanisms of feedback [that] have been part and parcel of higher education for a long time'. The campaign involved students in a range of activities to explore the feedback they received and the feedback they wanted. Over 3000 students were involved in focus groups, student networks, websites (including Facebook) and summer training sessions.

Principles for feedback were identified in order to address the issues raised by students in these activities concerning the timing and quality of feedback. Student attitudes towards feedback started with a positive appreciation (75 per cent) of how feedback provided information about performance, but then showed a decline for the statements 'feedback made it clear how to improve performance' (56 per cent), or 'motivated you to study' (54 per cent) (NUS 2009: 5.2).

The article from Porter in Box 5.1 rounds off this chapter with a clear statement on the principles of feedback that students want to underpin assessment.

Box 5.1 NUS – working to improve assessment feedback

By Aaron Porter, Vice President (Higher Education) NUS

This first edition focuses on feedback on assessment and builds on the work of the NUS Feedback Amnesty. It is clear that feedback on assessment is a fundamental part of the learning process. Not only does it enable students to develop and shape their learning but it can also foster greater levels of self-esteem and motivation. However, research results, such as those coming from the National Student Survey (NSS), the Higher Education Academy's Post-graduate Taught Experience Survey and NUS' own Student Experience Report, have all shown that poor assessment feedback procedures are a huge worry for students and, in some cases, having a negative impact on learning.

Complaints of ambiguity, lateness and negativity are commonplace in most university departments and the majority of students, 57% (NSS 2008), are not satisfied with the standard of feedback they are receiving. We are also seeing a stark variation in satisfaction with many disabled and minority ethnic students feeling they have a more negative experience of assessment feedback compared to their peers. This is a grave concern. Students are clearly being let down, and some more than others.

NUS has been addressing this issue over the last year. Our members have been vital in this work helping us create our ten principles of good feedback practice and informing us of the real-life experience that their members are facing. Our principles are as follows: NUS believes that feedback:

1   Should be for learning, not just of learning
    Feedback should be primarily used as a learning tool and therefore positioned for learning rather than as a measure of learning.
2   Should be a continuous process
    Rather than a one-off event after assessment, feedback should be part of continuous guided learning and an integral part of the learning experience.
3   Should be timely
    Feedback should be provided in a timely manner, allowing students to apply it to future learning and assessments. This timeframe needs to be communicated to students.
4   Should relate to clear criteria
    Objectives for assessment and grade criteria need to be clearly communicated to, and fully understood by, students. Subsequent feedback should be provided primarily in relation to this.
5   Should be constructive
    If feedback is to be constructive, it needs to be concise, focused and meaningful to feed-forward, highlighting what is going well and what can be improved.

6   Should be legible and clear
    Feedback should be written in plain language so it can be easily understood by all students, enabling them to engage with it and support future learning.
7   Should be provided on exams
    Exams make up a high proportion of assessment and students should receive feedback on how well they did and how they could improve for the next time.
8   Should include self-assessment and peer-to-peer feedback
    Feedback from peers and self-assessment practices can play a powerful role in learning by encouraging reassessment of personal beliefs and interpretations.
9   Should be accessible to all students
    Not all students are full-time, campus-based and so universities should utilise different technologies to ensure all students have easy access to their feedback.
10 Should be flexible and suited to students' needs
    Students learn in different ways and therefore feedback is not 'one size fits all'. Within reason students should be able to request feedback in various formats depending on their needs.
    Reproduced with permission: Porter, A. (2009) HE Focus 1(1): 1

Activity: Ten commandments – explore the ten principles and consider your practice

Are the principles likely to benefit student learning? For each one, ask what challenges you might face in responding to the principle.

Recommended follow-up reading

Bevan, R., Badge, J., Cann, A., Willmott, C. and Scott, J. (2008) Seeing eye-to-eye? Staff and student views on feedback. *Bioscience Education*, 12(1) http://www.bioscience.heacademy.ac.uk/journal/vol12/beej-12-1.aspx (accessed 4 August 2009).

Burke, D. (2009a) Strategies for using feedback that students bring to their degree course: an analysis of first year perceptions at the start of a course in Humanities. *Assessment and Evaluation in Higher Education*, 34(1): 41–50.

Weaver, M.R. (2006) Do students value feedback? Student perceptions of tutors' written response. *Assessment and Evaluation in Higher Education*, 31(3): 379–94.

6

Get set
Preparing students for written feedback

Many study skills texts aim to help students make a successful transition from school to university. Students are challenged by the study of new subjects, the complexity of referencing systems and the requirements of higher levels of analysis. Students also face a challenge in the type of feedback they will receive on their work in higher education. This chapter considers strategies to help students prepare for feedback on their work.

How far do the prior learning experiences of students prepare them for higher education? • Purposes of feedback in higher education • Attitudes to the role of feedback in learning • Understanding the assessment regime • Students preparing themselves for receiving and coping with judgements by others • Academic literacy: subject-specific induction • Workshops to prepare students for feedback • Recommended follow-up reading

Weaver's (2006: 379) study on student perceptions of tutors' written feedback found that 75 per cent of students had not received guidance on how to use feedback at university, and she concluded that students 'may need advice on understanding and using feedback before they can engage with it'. Wicklow (2009), the UK National Union of Students Academic Affairs Officer, can be seen to support this conclusion in her recommendation that students are provided with the 'tools' to use feedback from the start of their course. The aim of this chapter is to explore ways to prepare students for the feedback they will receive on their work by giving them such tools.

This exploration links to the ASK approach to learning, developed by Burke and Pieterick, which seeks to bring a change in attitudes (A) to study to prevent early closure; this is supported by introducing students to a range of strategies (S) for learning, leading to knowledge (K) both cognitive and practical to guide student learning. This chapter explores the cognitive aspects of this approach while the next chapter explores practical strategies for students to use in unpacking and acting on tutor feedback. The ASK approach encourages students to develop their attitude to tutor comments, so that they are seen to go beyond feedback on past work to feedforward into future learning. With regard to knowledge, students gain the cognitive perspective that feedback is integral to their learning as it provides evidence of their achievement and indicates areas for development.

How far do the prior learning experiences of students prepare them for higher education?

Ecclestone's (2007: 41) report on entry point research with students provides a useful framework from which to consider student starting points. In particular he stated we 'need to understand more about the ways in which students' previous experiences of assessment shape their expectations, attitudes and effectiveness in engaging with different methods and approaches'. This chapter considers expectations and attitudes towards feedback, while Chapter 7 focuses on effectiveness in engaging with feedback. Earlier chapters explored the vast research, advice and guidance for tutors on approaches to feedback. This maze is difficult for experts in the field to navigate, let alone novice students, thus this chapter explores where students are coming from and the implications arising from such starting points.

Burke's induction survey (2009a) with humanities and social science students revealed understandings of feedback that students held from previous study experiences. The majority of students (69 per cent) indicated a positive view of the feedback and an awareness of the ways that it enhanced their learning. Only 6 per cent disagreed, while about a quarter had variable experiences of feedback, some good and some bad. Those who found feedback useful identified a number of ways that written feedback had enhanced their learning. These statements from students show their expectations about feedback, some of which may be realized in higher education, but others that may not due to assessment strategies; thus, students need to adjust their expectations. Prior preparation is necessary to help students align their expectations for feedback to current practices in higher education.

The following activity invites you to think about the types of comments you tend to use in your feedback, and then takes you on to compare your categories with those identified by students.

Activity: Categorize your comments

You can either do this as a guesstimate or work from five scripts. Break your comments into the following areas identified by Hyatt's survey of tutor comments.

Hyatt's categories	Your profile
Phatic: comments to help you build a relationship with the student.	
Developmental: comments to help the student develop their work, offering alternatives and things to think about for the future.	
Structural: comments relating to the coherence of units, sentences, paragraphs or the whole assignment.	
Stylistic: concerning grammatical issues and referencing.	
Content: comments evaluating the accuracy and appropriateness of subject content.	
Method and Administration: comments referring to the research method underpinning the work, and the requirements of the task.	

Activity: Compare your categories

Fill in your categories in Table 6.1 and consider where you stand in relation to the findings from the tutor and student research.

Two main points stand out from Table 6.1: first, over half of the students at induction stated the expectation that tutor feedback would be developmental, yet only a quarter of tutor comments in Hyatt's study *were* developmental. Conversely few students expected comments on the content of their essay, yet Hyatt's study suggested this to be the category most used by

Table 6.1 Feedback categories

Categories	Tutor comments Hyatt 2005 (%)	Student Responses Burke 2009a (%)	Your % use of these categories
Phatic	3	2	
Developmental	23	53	
Structural	8	15	
Stylistic	27	25	
Content	32	5	
Method and Administration	7	0	

tutors. This suggests that students entering higher education are likely to face a steep learning curve as they encounter feedback which focuses more on subject content than on their individual development. Thus, some clarification for students on the types of comment to expect in higher education would prepare them for the feedback they are likely to receive.

Haines (2004: 22) listed seven types of assessor comments which have different roles for learning and different impacts on student learning. Thus, an activity which took students through these different types of comment would help students to make more sense of feedback when they received it. Initial student responses to feedback in higher education may be emotive and induce a feeling that there is too much criticism, whereas an unpacking of the different types of comments might show the student that advisory comments and rhetorical questions are aimed at improving their work. While other comments may be positive in praising or noting correct aspects of work, there is still the need to work through corrective comments that provide regulatory instruction or direct criticism. If students are aware of the benefit that such comments can have for their academic journey, it may be easier to take them on board.

Purposes of feedback in higher education

At the start of this section it is worth breaking off for a moment to explore the purposes that you intend feedback on work to have for your students.

Activity: Four feedback truths – your view of the purposes of feedback

Now compare your purposes with those below, considering if you agree with that purpose or not, and how you would rank the purposes.

- to justify the mark awarded;
- to show how far learning outcomes have been achieved;
- to comment on the development of subject academic literacy (planning, style, referencing);
- to motivate the student by praising achievements in the work;
- to identify areas that the student needs to develop;
- to suggest resources for the development of student learning;
- to explain why aspects are correct and worthy of praise;
- to explain why aspects are not appropriate and show what *would* be an appropriate expression;
- to identify the gap between current performance and desired performance at that level of study.

Attitudes to the role of feedback in learning

The ASK approach is based on students developing an understanding of the central role that written feedback plays in their learning journey. The complexity of learning tasks in higher education requires expert external feedback to help students monitor their progress within their subject discipline. Prosser and Webb (1994: 136) recommended a holistic approach in which students were able to link process and product: 'Students need to be systematically helped to reflect on, and change, their understanding of the nature of the task in the context in which the task is undertaken.' The first step is for students to develop their effectiveness in engaging with different methods and approaches to feedback. Most subjects in higher education use feedback proforma or rubric to ensure consistency in the form of feedback students receive. Introducing the proforma to students before they hand in their first assignment can help students focus on the aspects of the task to be scrutinized in tutor feedback. This example of a feedback proforma with explanations sets out information to help the student understand the mechanics of the feedback process (see Box 6.1). This can link to workshops later in this chapter which introduce students to examples of marked work.

In the critical moment when students receive their feedback, foresight of the feedback proforma and prior preparation can help them 'read' the comments in a more appropriate manner. Studies such as Haines (2004) which chart the different types of comments can help students become aware of the different facets of feedback comments. Numerous studies with students report the tendency, when receiving marked work, for them to focus on the grade and overlook the feedback. Thus, any form of preparation that encourages students to look beyond the grade to the tutor comments and their implications is a

Box 6.1 Feedback proforma with explanation

Student Number: *Use only your student number, do not include your name as we follow a policy on anonymous marking.*

Module code and title:

Task: Specify the task as this helps you to ensure that you have focused on the set task.

Learning outcomes: *Set out the specific learning outcomes for this task.*

	Feedback	Feedforward
Referencing: *use of sources, referencing, your bibliography*	This section feeds back on how far your work review met these requirements.	This section offers suggestions for your future improvement. This may include hyperlinks to resources that help you develop your skills and understanding.
Structure: *relevance, understanding of task and organization of material*		
Style/mechanics: *clarity of expression, appropriate spelling and grammar*		
Content: *your selection of relevant content to present your interesting section*		

Overall comment: **Grade:** *Refer to the Grade Point Scale to interpret your grade.*

Your tutor will provide comments which pull together all the comments made on your script and in the feedback section above. This comment will aim to provide a balanced account of your achievements in the essay.

Please read through this feedback and comments on your essay before signing up for a tutorial. *You can book a tutorial to discuss the feedback with your tutor.*

Marker: **Date:**   **Moderator:**

All batches of scripts are subject to moderation. If there is a signature, it shows your script was one of those monitored.

Staff recommendation: main area for you to work on

This section helps you to prioritize your efforts by highlighting the main point from the feedback. This can help you take the first step for acting on feedback.

Student action: *make a note of your intentions on reading this feedback*

This section is for you to complete when you have thought about this feedback. Make a record of your thoughts so you can put them into action before you start on your next assignment.

move in the right direction. It can help students move beyond the academic judgement in the tutor comment to think about the basis for the judgement, and start to think about what actions to take to address the issue in the tutor comment.

A good place to start student preparation is Butler and Winne's (1995: 246) proposed five functions of feedback, as they are specifically related to subject academic understanding and application. They justify this approach in this statement:

> We believe broader scope, deeper analysis, and a reviewing of the temporal location of feedback's effects are necessary to capture feedback's roles in knowledge construction. To acknowledge feedback's multiple and multifaceted roles in learning, we position feedback within a model of self-regulation that guides cognitive activities during which knowledge is accreted, tuned, and restructured.

The identification of these five functions provides a useful framework to use with students to help them develop a broader understanding of feedback on their work. The functions are as follows: to draw attention to clashes between conceptual understandings and the goals of the task; to provide additional information; to identify where prior knowledge held by the student is inappropriate for the task; to help students 'tune their understandings and discriminate between concepts'; and finally, if the student is holding false theories, feedback will identify the need 'to restructure schemata' (Butler and Winne 1995: 246). The list, as they presented it, only deals with the types of corrections that tutors make on work, but this focus on deficiency can be turned round to recognize achievement in these areas.

Thus prior preparation of students for such a model of feedback can help students understand the types of areas that tutor comments are likely to refer to. Box 6.2 illustrates how this list of five functions is used to prepare students for an introductory task in Religious Studies of comparing an insider presentation of Sikhism with the presentation in a textbook.

Box 6.2 Five functions example

In this assignment you need to use information from the field visit to the Gurdwara to discuss points of similarity and difference with the presentation of Sikhism in a textbook. You are required to explore reasons for the differences. In marking, attention will be given to your use of material to engage with this set task. It is likely that feedback comments will cover the following areas:

The first area concerns the *conceptual understandings* you hold in relation to the methods used to study aspects of religion.

Secondly, feedback will consider if your work is *lacking in essential information*, so feedback will check that you have provided details from the class field visit to the Gurdwara, details from your selected text book as well as issues raised on methods to study religion.

Thirdly, feedback will address any *assumptions that you make on the basis of prior knowledge* that are inappropriate for this task. You need to approach the task in a phenomenological manner, bracketing out your prior assumptions, so that you focus on the material under consideration. This task may be particularly difficult if you bring prior insider knowledge of Sikhism, as you are not required to provide your knowledge of Sikhism but to compare the two sources under consideration.

Fourthly, feedback will explore how well you have dealt with the *complexity of academic knowledge*; in particular you need to address 'theories' that seek to explain differences between insider (emic) and outsider (etic) viewpoints.

Finally, feedback will help you '*restructure schemata*' if your work suggests that there are aspects of the underpinning theories of phenomenology and the study of religion that you seem to have misunderstood.

Activity: Be prepared – preparing students for your feedback

Explore your subject and module literature to see what guidance is provided for students on feedback.

- Do they know what kind of feedback to expect?
- Do they know what to do with your feedback?
- Do you provide suggestions for tutorial, literature or electronic support?

How have students thought of themselves as a learner? What prior experiences have shaped their expectations about tutor feedback?

Understanding the assessment regime

An essential part of unpacking feedback requires students to relate feedback on their work to the set learning outcomes and assessment criteria. Acting on feedback requires the development of an element of objectivity; the ability to stand back from one's own work and see it from another's perspective. Institutional personal development planning initiatives seek to develop independent, analytic learners, but research (Weaver 2006; MacLellan 2001) suggests that students often do not make the conceptual connection between feedback and their own development.

One major difference between students' past experiences and the framework for learning in many higher education institutions is semesterized modularity, which concentrates learning into a short period. This move to a system whereby teaching, learning and assessment are completed within a semester is a change for new students. Whereas, in the past, student study was linked in a year-long course, modularity appears to encourage students to compartmental-ize their learning. Students often consider module feedback to be so specific that it is only relevant to the particular essay, and they do not think that it informs future learning. Irons noted this student disengagement from the formative aspects of summative assessment, seeming to hold the view that 'formative feedback on end-of-module summative assessments adds no value to their future modules' (2008: 16).

The move to new modules each semester, often with different members of staff, can fragment learning. Colleagues found this module content-focused view to be a reason why students did not bother to pick up their marked essays to receive feedback (Winter and Dye 2005). Thus, there is a challenge to prepare students for modularity to ensure that learning experiences in one module are carried forward to other modules.

Activity: Linking feedback across modules

List the ways in which you help students make links.

Personal marking to anonymous marking

Students in the induction survey (Burke 2009a) showed they had appreciated the personalized feedback provided by teachers. Most teachers had taught them over a period of years and they had developed a good relationship with them. Hyatt (2005) identified phatic as a category in tutor comments, whose purpose is to develop a relationship with the student and personalize the feedback, rather than convey any particular information about student performance. Developing such a relationship can be difficult because of the tutor:student ratios operating in higher education. Also it may be the case that students meet tutors for one module only which militates against tutors drawing attention to personal development in their marking. In addition, many universities have moved to a system of anonymous marking. This means that tutors mark the work in front of them without any consideration of the person behind the work. Thus, comments tend not to attempt to develop a relationship with the student or draw attention to the particular achievement of the actual student in relation to their past learning.

Activity: Anonymous marking – how do you cope?

List the differences between personal and anonymous marking.
What are the implications for students of this change?

Strategies to personalize anonymously marked assignments are set out in later chapters on feedback tutorials and personal tutor tutorials.

Students preparing themselves for receiving and coping with judgements by others

The earlier chapter on student perspectives on feedback revealed student anxieties about the judgemental aspect of feedback, which Yorke (2002) suggested could result in student drop-out. Weaver's (2006) survey reported that over 90 per cent of students found that positive comments boosted their confidence, and Weaver drew attention to Young's (cited in Weaver 2006: 382) findings that: 'High and medium self-esteem students tended to see feedback as something they were able to act on and make use of.' So far so good, but she continues that 'students with low self-esteem were more likely to feel defeated and consider leaving the course'.

Here we consider ways to ease this anxiety by preparing students before they receive feedback on their work. Boud and Falchikov (2007: 154) recommend preparation so that students find it easier to receive and cope with judgements made on their work. They state: 'learners should be helped to prepare themselves for receiving and coping with judgements by others through understanding the assessment regime to which they are subject'.

The first challenge is to avoid subjectification: 'A big problem occurs when one party (the teacher) objectifies all their judgements, and the other party (the student) subjectifies all theirs' (Boud and Falchikov 2007: 154). Many students respond emotionally to feedback by taking negative comments as a personal judgement on their capabilities as a student. This tendency to subjectify, to take comments personally, may mean that their emotional response reduces their capacity to respond to the comment. They can only see the negativity in the comment, for example, 'you showed a good understanding of the key issues but did not use this understanding to explore the issues raised by the question'. This tendency to overlook valuable feedback and focus only on the negative aspects of feedback, means that in this instance the student may not have noticed the academic judgement that they have developed a 'good understanding of the key issues'.

Encouraging students to explore Dweck's self-theories of intelligence (1999) can help them develop their objectivity. Those holding an entity view of intelligence tend to possess a fixed view of intelligence as something that does not change. Thus, they are likely to interpret comments about performance on a piece of work as a judgement on them as a person. Thus, comments that they have failed a task will be taken to mean that they personally are failures. Dweck recommends that students develop an incremental view of intelligence, where learning tasks are seen as opportunities to develop. Such students have less to fear from failure, and understand learning to be a journey rather than a destination.

Academic literacy: subject-specific induction

Higgins et al.'s (2001) exploration of the problems communicating assessment feedback in 'Getting the message across', specified that feedback should be understood as a 'unique form of communication'. However, students need to be initiated into this communication to ensure that they 'conceptualize' feedback in the way intended by the tutor. Weaver (2006: 380) also drew attention to the importance of shared understandings, noting 'students who do not yet share a similar understanding of academic discourse as the tutor would subsequently have difficulty in understanding and using the feedback'. Thus, students need to be prepared for the feedback they will receive and know what to do with it when it arrives. Higgins et al. recommend that tutors prepare students for assessment by 'feeding forward into a piece of work'. Preparing students for the academic terms that are central to a discipline will ensure that students are more likely to understand tutor comments that use such academic terms. Students use, and understanding of key terms help to facilitate their wider initiation into a subject's academic literacy.

Northedge compares the task facing students to the idea of a novice joining a community. This idea of the student as a novitiate or apprentice is interesting as it conveys the way that students learn by doing, with the exception that the assessments on their practice are summative and affect their overall profile as a learner. Northedge (2003: 78) explores the issue of novices who 'are expected to speak, write and criticize in the new discourse'. Such discourses are complex, involving 'tacit' knowledge, where subtle meanings are teased out and elaborated through written assessments. This challenge is further complicated when the student's prior educational experiences are different from the academic community they join in higher education.

Moore et al.'s (2010) study skills text includes a section on 'learning how to get the most out of experts'. This chapter suggests ways for students to navigate the novice- expert divide, and while there is no specific mention of conversations with tutors about feedback on assignments, some of the activities would help students develop confidence in their encounters with tutors.

This challenge can be illustrated by Paxton's (1998: 150) study from the perspective of economics, where students are required to move from a general understanding of economic discourse, such as that found in the media, to the alien abstract academic discourse used by the subject. This transition starts with the process of acquisition, by which discourses are acquired through interaction with 'experts who have mastered the discourse'. He notes that feedback is a crucial part of this process, which should lead to students passing through the phase of acquisition to learning. Such feedback should be 'clear and constructive' so that the 'learning process is to be productive' (1998: 151).

Activity: Subject preparation for feedback

Has this section prompted you to think about ways of preparing students for aspects of assessed work that they find difficult?
List the possible difficulties and ways to respond.

Workshops to prepare students for feedback

Students who have been used to personalized feedback in their prior school or college learning experiences may be surprised by the formal academic feedback they receive at university. They can be helped to make this transition to higher education practices by using study skills texts, prompt materials and subject-specific workshops.

Study skills texts provide practical advice for students that could be used in workshops. Much of the information is general to skills in higher education rather than specific to the unpacking and acting on tutor feedback. Moore et al. (2010) provide a useful section on 'Talking to experts', and while this advice focuses on asking questions within lectures and seminars, the skills developed could help students approach their tutors to explore feedback on their work.

McMillan and Weyers (2009) provide advice that can be used to prepare students for feedback, or help them work through feedback they have received. They offer three main suggestions for students. First, to be 'mentally prepared' to learn from the tutor's comments, so that expert insight can inform learning in the subject. Second, to 'understand the feedback', talking to peers or tutors to clarify feedback comments. Finally, to take all feedback on board from all modules studied, not just those from the main subject.

Workshops based around past student assignments with tutor feedback on them can be used to help students prepare for feedback. Students can be set particular tasks in pairs or small groups, working from examples of marked student work. This could be a progressive activity, working from aspects of feedback they have been used to in the past, such as grammatical corrections, before they move on to more complex aspects of academic writing. Specific issues concerning tutor feedback could be drawn from a selection of your past marked essays, to allow students to see the kinds of comments you are likely to provide on their work. Students could then explore issues noted in feedback comments to skills guides. McMillan and Weyers (2009: 378–9) provide a useful table in their 'Common types of feedback annotation and how to act in response'. This table provides a range of comments that tutors are likely to make and guidance for students on how to work out what the tutor annotations mean, and what the annotations require students to do. In relation to content, for example, they include 'too descriptive' as a typical tutor comment, and guide the student to the meaning of this term and potential remedial action: 'it may be that your work lacks substance and you appear to have compensated by putting in too much description rather than analysis, for example' (2009: 378).

This approach helps students develop objectivity and allows them to explore feedback without their emotions colouring and curtailing their reading. Such practised readings of feedback can help students develop good habits in reading feedback, which they can draw on when they receive feedback on their own work.

Finally, assignments could be returned to the whole class during a lecture session, with a verbal reminder to students on the key aspects of the task, how marks were arrived at and some general unpacking of terms used in feedback. This approach would ensure that students were not left alone with feedback that they might misinterpret.

Activity: Exploring achievement of learning outcomes

Remind students of the task and the learning outcomes they were expected to demonstrate.
Remind students of the assessment criteria used for marking, and the grading system. Often students misinterpret grades and think they may have failed with, say, a D grade, when it is a pass grade.

One way forward is to help students develop their 'metacognitive skills' so they are able to apply their generic and study skills in new situations, and draw upon feedback experiences to regulate their learning (Biggs 2003). There are hints in earlier studies to show how feedback can help in the process of development. Race 1994 set out his 'ripple model' to demonstrate the messy nature of learning, where making mistakes is a necessary part of the learning journey. If students are able to gain this perspective of learning as involving trial and error, then they are more likely to regard feedback on an essay as a stage in this journey rather than a destination.

Recommended follow-up reading

Orrell, J. (2006) Feedback on learning achievement: rhetoric and reality. *Teaching in Higher Education*, 11(4): 441–56.
Race, P. (1995) What has assessment done for us – and to us? In P. Knight (ed.) *Assessment for Learning in Higher Education*. London: Kogan Page, pp. 61–74.

7

Strategies for students to get more out of feedback

This chapter explores a range of strategies that students can use to unpack tutor feedback, prepare for a tutorial with their tutor, get more out of a tutorial, and finally develop a learner action plan to act on the feedback.

Working on feedback • Feedback tutorial • Tutorial discussion • Feedback tutorial template • Learner Action Plan • Acting on feedback: suggestions • Summary • Recommended follow-up reading

The range of strategies set out in this chapter build on Gibbs and Simpson's (2004) principles to help student response to feedback:

- Feedback is received by students and attended to.
- Feedback is acted upon by students to improve their work or their learning.

Activity: Do as I say, not as I did – how did you respond to feedback?

Think back to when you were a student. What actions can you remember taking on tutor feedback?

Comments	Your response/follow-up

If I am honest, I cannot remember doing much with feedback. Part of the reason lay in the feedback I received; mostly cryptic comments that did not offer much by way advice for development. I recall one comment on my planning: 'you seem to approach essay writing as if you were playing darts, hoping that if you throw enough darts at the board you will eventually hit bull's-eye'. This was a memorable comment, as evidenced by the fact than I can remember it some 35 years later, but it was not a comment that I could really act on.

In my induction survey (Burke 2009a) just over a third of students (39 per cent) stated that they had been given guidance on how to use written feedback at their prior institution, with the rest either having been given no guidance (46 per cent) or 'part' guidance (15 per cent). Overall a majority remembered being given some guidance, but for some students guidance was merely to read the comments. Weaver's (2006) study found that 50 per cent of students had not received guidance during the course of their undergraduate study. These statistics are quite surprising; do we expect students to know what to do with our feedback without giving them any guidance? This chapter attempts to tackle this challenge by setting out a range of strategies for students to use to get more out of tutor feedback on their work.

Activity: What do you think students do with your feedback on their work?

Consider the question and answer honestly. Which of the following do you expect?

- read it when they get their work back
- plan to act on the feedback
- come to a tutorial to discuss issues raised
- read books on study skills to address issues
- other actions

In the previous chapter we noted the characteristics of feedback as part of a process to induct novice students into academic literacy within their subject discipline. If we turn now to consider the challenge for such novices, Carless (2007) identified three main factors in tutor feedback. First, feedback assesses student achievement of learning outcomes and indicates areas for further development of points. Second, the feedback should explain the basis on which judgements about performance had been made in a straightforward manner, so that students can use this information. Finally, the feedback should lead to action by the student. Thus, it is clear that in order for all three factors to be realized, students need to be able to unpack and interpret tutor feedback. In the previous chapter it was noted that the complexity of the judgements made by tutors in feedback requires careful reading by students to discern its meaning. Rust (2002) has drawn attention to research findings which suggest that feedback's impact on student learning will be limited unless students engage actively with the feedback.

The purpose of this chapter is both proactive and reactive: proactive in seeking to improve the use that students already make of tutor feedback, and reactive as a response to the minimal student engagement with feedback. The problem of student failure to use feedback has been around a long time, as noted by Knoblauch and Brannon (1981: 1), who claimed there is 'scarcely a shred of empirical evidence to show that students typically even comprehend our responses to their writing, let alone use them purposefully to modify their practice'. Has this situation changed? Would you be surprised if the date for the quote was 2010?

Let us pause to consider these two elements of student engagement with feedback: to understand tutor comments, and then to act on the advice. How can we strengthen this important link between tutor feedback and student learning, so that feedback becomes a central learning resource for students? The 'Using Feedback Effectively' form (a full copy is available at the end of this chapter) was developed from a cross-university workshop at Wolverhampton, UK. The form presents a Using Feedback Effectively strategy to support students in their interaction with tutor feedback. Initial feedback from students has been very positive, as identified by this student comment: 'This exercise was interesting and helpful to complete. I had misunderstood some feedback I received and if I had not completed this exercise I would have continued doing what I was doing wrong, which would have had a negative impact on my work' (in Burke 2007a).

The three stages of the Using Feedback Effectively strategy link to MacLellan's (2001) research on tutor and student perceptions on feedback, addressing the 'detail' in feedback, openings for discussion with tutors, and how feedback can improve learning. Stage one of the Using Feedback Effectively strategy explores issues concerning the detail of feedback; stage two explores how to promote discussion between student and tutor; and stage three focuses on how to encourage students to take action on feedback so that they learn from it. The overall aim of changes is to address MacLellan's (2001: 316) perception that 'most students did not view feedback on their learning as either routinely helpful in itself or as a catalyst for discussion'.

Working on feedback

Students are likely to write fewer assignments during a degree course than they did in their previous study, so it is important that they glean all they can from the feedback they receive. At school or college, teachers were able to provide regular personalized feedback to assist individual development. Anonymous marking schemes and the anonymity of studying in large groups at university often place students in a new position in relation to the feedback they receive. They are likely to receive feedback less frequently; it may look more formal on official feedback forms; and it may be phrased in an academic language that students are only starting to learn. Whatever the reasons, Carless (2007: 47) reports the tendency among students 'to give written feedback, no matter how carefully composed, only cursory attention'. This stage takes students back to the feedback on their essay, and encourages them to work carefully through certain points to see how far they have achieved the learning outcomes, and to access advice from tutors on how to develop. Their task may be complicated by our use of academic jargon or personal codes, which can be idiosyncratic and difficult to interpret. Students need to work through the feedback line by line, and to link tutor comments to specific sections of their essay and to marking criteria.

Activity: Unpacking comments – stage 1

Give students a copy of the Using Feedback Effectively form with the feedback on their work, and ask them to complete the first section with the following instruction:

Read the feedback on your assignment carefully, then re-read the piece of work to see the areas that the feedback refers to. You might use a highlighter pen to cross-refer the feedback to your work, or to draw attention to corrections and suggestions.

Then select two tutor comments and show what you understand these to mean.

What has your tutor written?	What do you understand this to mean?
You should make more use of the quotations you include.	*I understand this to mean that when I include a quote I should draw out the implications that the quote has for my essay. The quote might back up the point*

What has your tutor written?	What do you understand this to mean?
	I am making, or it might offer a different perspective so I can use it as a jumping off point for the next part of my essay. In either case I need to make explicit reference to my reason for including the quote.

Breaking feedback down into positives and negatives

Earlier chapters explored the emotional impact of feedback on students and suggested ways to prepare students to cope with feedback. Often feedback can seem totally negative to students: pointing out spelling or grammatical mistakes, factual errors, questioning their interpretations and specifying the need to reference correctly. Taking negative points on board is very difficult, and students may be inclined not to read the feedback if it is perceived to be negative.

However, it is important they read through the feedback carefully and make a note of all comments, to accrue the benefits identified by this student: 'I feel it is important to be aware that you are good at certain things. I used to have a tendency to look at the negative points made and therefore have a negative view of my abilities. I now realize the criticism I receive is for me to use to my advantage' (in Burke 2007a).

Activity: Unpacking comments – stage 2, the good and the ugly

Ask students to identify three good points and three areas for improvement from your feedback using the following format.

Good points (note them so you can do them again)	Areas for improvement (draw out main areas from feedback)

Race (2001: 4) offers an interesting perspective on this process of recognizing positives and negatives. He refers to two categories of 'uncompetence' that may be identified through tutor feedback. First, conscious uncompetence refers to aspects that students already know they cannot do. Race holds that the fact that this uncompetence is conscious means that students are receptive to acting in relation to the thing they realize they cannot do. However, the most important learning for students concerns unconscious uncompetence; this helps 'students find out much more about what they didn't yet know that they couldn't yet do' (p. 4). Race presents learning as a journey through boxes. Starting with the 'danger box', the position of unconscious uncompetence, tutor feedback can help students exit this box and move to the 'transit box' that indicates conscious uncompetence. Once students enter this box they possess the awareness to work on an aspect of their learning, and this motivation helps their journey towards the 'target box'.

However, learning from feedback is not limited to learning about uncompetence. Race also identifies two aspects of competence. Conscious competence is the target awareness for the student; this knowledge of how they completed the task successfully will enable them to replicate this competence in the future. Unconscious competence is the hidden gem of feedback, as it reveals to students their success in areas they did not know they could do well. This new knowledge of developing competence is important for student self-knowledge, as it will increase confidence and motivation for future tasks.

Initial reading of feedback that includes some negatives may mean that students miss positive points. It is just as important that students note their successes, as these are the things they need to continue to do in the future. This recording of positives is also important to counteract the tendency to dwell on negatives. One workshop participant noted: 'I concentrated on positives, only because we were *told* to, my instinct was to look for negatives' (in Burke 2005). Such a systematic overview enables the student to take a balanced account of their achievements, in order to counter Race's (1997: 64) observation that students 'often are quite blind to valuable feedback'.

This activity will help students take a balanced view of feedback, recording both the things they have done well and the areas for improvement. This first stage may enable students to get what they need out of feedback. They can use this summary of the feedback as a record for their personal development planning, and maintain a learning portfolio across all modules. Students will then be in a position to see if all the tutors are saying the same thing or to consider if there are things they have done well in one module that could be applied to other areas.

However, the complexity of the issues raised by tutor feedback may mean that many students need to go further and that they will benefit from discussion with their tutor. Students may be puzzled about terms used by tutors, or it may be the case that students are unsure where they stand due to the brevity of tutor feedback.

Feedback tutorial

This aspect of the strategy may not be feasible due to pressures on tutor time. Parts of the process could be used without the option of a tutorial, but obviously the student would get more from an actual tutorial. Skills tutors have proved to be an important link in helping students prepare for a tutorial with their tutor, as indicated in Case Study 8 (see pp. 143–7).

Carless's (2007) research identified the benefits arising from discussion in helping students understand the feedback and its relation to assessment criteria, he reported that for students the opportunity to discuss the feedback made learning more effective. However, Carless also noted some student reluctance in seeking tutorials. He reported: 'But when asked if they took the initiative to approach lecturers, they invariably said that they did not' (2007: 226). Why are students reluctant to approach lecturers?

Lack of confidence is a major reason for reluctance. Students who have low self-esteem will find it difficult to discuss negative comments on their work with tutors. Such students may find it easier to put feedback sheets, which they regard as negative, out of sight and out of mind. Thus, if having an essay tutorial is a matter of choice, it can be easy for students to opt out of facing up to perceived failings by not having one (Orrell 2006). However, when a tutorial is required, students have to face up to the feedback, and through this process can gain a balanced overview of their achievements to direct future learning.

MacLellan's (2001) findings on the gap between staff and student perceptions of feedback revealed the greatest discrepancy in response to the question 'how far feedback prompted discussion between tutor and student'. Tutors responded that feedback 'frequently' prompts discussion, but who they had discussion with is questionable as 50 per cent of students stated feedback 'never' prompted discussion!

Preparation for a tutorial

This section of the Using Feedback Effectively form responds to these findings by providing support for student discussion with tutors. This stage of preparation is important to ensure that students get the most out of tutorial opportunities. In many cases feedback tutorials consist of the tutor taking the essay from the student, reading the comments they have made, and then telling the student what they should do. (This links to Chapter 3 on revision control.) This type of encounter maintains the power relationship between tutor and student, and holds the student in a passive role. Rarely do students come in with questions about the feedback, and if they do ask questions, there is a tendency for these to be framed in an emotive or accusative manner.

Thus, this stage of preparation, and the use of an agreed template, can empower the student to use the opportunity to ask the questions they want to about the feedback and their essay performance in an appropriate manner.

This 'reframing' of the tutorial process follows Boud's recommendation to go beyond seeing students as 'passive recipients of feedback' (in Boud and Falchikov 2007).

The use of a form for this activity acts to legitimize students asking questions about the feedback. This process of students asking questions about what a tutor meant by a comment can be problematic if students are thought to be challenging tutor judgements. Race et al. (2005) note a number of disadvantages in face-to-face feedback settings, including the issue of 'defensiveness' by both parties. Yet for any learning to take place, students need to understand tutor comments and think about how to act on them. Thinking about the question in advance and writing out the questions may help students frame questions in a manner that tutors do not find challenging, and thus enable students to take this important step in finding out what the tutor meant.

Activity: Please sir? Helping students prepare for a tutorial

Invite students to complete the 'Preparation for a tutorial' section of the form, using the following instructions:

Use these prompts to prepare for a tutorial with your module tutor.

Make an appointment with your tutor and take this form and your assignment to the tutorial.

Feedback that you understand	Fill in the actions you intend to take on these points and discuss with your tutor
You should make more use of the quotations you include.	I understand this to mean that when I include a quote I should draw out the implications that the quote has for my essay. The quote might back up the point I am making, or it might offer a different perspective so I can use it as a jumping off point for the next part of my essay. In either case I need to make explicit reference to my reason for including the quote.

The form recommends that students start with comments they think they understand, and use the opportunity to check that their interpretation of tutor comments is correct. This gives students a chance to show the tutor that they have taken the time to read through the feedback and think about the implications of tutor comments. This checking of understanding by the student is important as we noted Higgins et al.'s (2001) contention that feedback is a complex form of communication.

The move to feedback comments students do not understand, then, takes place when the student has gained some confidence from discussing straightforward comments. This provides a foundation for students to ask the more difficult questions about the tutor comments they do not understand. Requesting clarification on the meaning of a term used by the tutor, or challenging a statement in the feedback is more difficult for students. By thinking about how to word their question in advance, students may phrase their request in a manner that makes it easier for their tutor to reply. In many cases the issue will be about a comment that the student may not understand in relation to their essay. This could be because they think they have completed a task, while the feedback suggests they have not. Thus, discussion is required to appreciate that their engagement with the task may have been partial. So, for example, the student may be thinking the tutor comment, 'apply Smart's theory to this situation', is strange because they used Smart. But it could be that the student summarized parts of Smart's theory, but did not apply it to the example under consideration. Only discussion can clear up this scenario, the student thinking that the comment is wrong because they did use Smart and not seeing beyond this feeling of injustice. Referring back to Butler and Winne's five functions of feedback reminds us of the complexity of the feedback process. Discussion can help clarify situations to see that comments need to be interpreted as a matter of degree rather than categorical statements.

Feedback you do not understand	Fill this column in during the tutorial
'more critical reflection needed'	My tutor said in the tutorial that I tend to write descriptively and do not draw out the impact of each piece of information for the question I was exploring.

Students who lack confidence may find it easier to discuss the feedback with a skills tutor in advance of a tutorial with their subject tutor. This preparation can help students clarify the issues for discussion on essay feedback and they may also find it useful to get help with the phrasing of questions. Some students may find such preparation or rehearsal helps to build their confidence. (Details about the role of skills tutors in helping students get more out of tutor feedback are explored in Chapter 8.)

Tutorial discussion

This asking of questions enables the student to enter into dialogue with the tutor, and empowers the student to take control of the revision process. This opportunity to discuss how far they were successful in communicating their intentions is a vital step. As Brannon and Knoblauch (1982: 162, original emphasis) noted: 'Writers know what they *intended* to communicate. Readers know what a text has *actually* said to them.' Thus, the tutor can fulfil the role of a 'sounding board', enabling the student to see where their communication was successful and where it needs revision. This step empowers the student through dialogue: 'By negotiating those changes rather than dictating them, the teacher returns control of the writing to the student' (Sommers 1982: 149).

The opportunity to discuss their assignment with a tutor enables a student to engage in academic discourse, which is necessarily complex when exploring ideas and arguments. Such dialogue serves to initiate students into subject-specific academic discourse, as noted by Higgins et al.: 'Discussion, clarification and negotiation between student and tutor can equip students with a better appreciation of what is expected of them, and develop their understandings of academic terms and appropriate practices' (2001: 27).

We noted Butler and Winne's (1995) five functions of feedback in an earlier section, and it is probable that some of these functions are only likely to be achieved in a discursive situation where the student seeks more information from the tutor about comments in feedback. First, the students can explore comments relating to their understanding of key concepts in the work. Second, the student can discuss the tutor suggestions for sections which required more information. Third, the student can discuss the tutor's view on how elements of prior knowledge influenced the student's interpretations in the essay. Fourth, students can use discussions to 'refine' their understandings of key concepts. Finally, students can challenge tutor perceptions of false theories held by the student to gain an understanding of how these theories are incompatible with subject knowledge.

Students (in Burke 2007a) noted that this process of discussion with the tutor enabled them to explore feedback that seemed contradictory. One student noted a comment on the script, 'set out your views in an objective manner', while the feedback sheet noted 'You are developing a strong personal voice'. On the surface these comments seem to conflict and confused the recipient. Clarity is only likely to be achieved through a tutorial, where the student can ask questions and enter into dialogue with the tutor and ask the meaning of each comment.

Students also drew attention to the fact that the process, with use of a specific form, allows for 'legitimate questioning of feedback by students'. One student identified the benefits gained from a feedback tutorial: 'It was a good opportunity to discuss strengths and weaknesses, which we do not always have the opportunity to do because once the work is marked I'm thinking ahead to the next essay and don't act on the feedback.'

Feedback tutorial template

This section explores the use of a Word template by subject tutors to record discussion from a tutorial, and offer follow-up advice. The template was originally designed for use by skills tutors, to enable them to send a record of the tutorial discussion to students. (More detailed exploration of this template can be found in Chapter 8 and Case Study 8.)

The main purpose of the tutorial template is to provide a record of the discussion. Race et al. (2005: 120) noted that students will find it difficult to remember all the discussion. In particular they noted: 'Students often tend to remember only *some* of a feedback interview . . . often the most critical element, and this may undermine confidence unduly.' The record of discussion will provide a focus on the main learning aspect discussed. In addition, the use of the Word template enables tutors to provide hyperlinks to follow-up electronic materials.

The provision of hyperlinks has the advantage of anytime anyplace accessibility for students. Research by Weaver (2006) noted that only 4 per cent of students surveyed consulted study skills texts for guidance in following up feedback. Hyperlinks take students directly to suggested materials, rather than leaving them to plough through sections of a book.

Feedback tutorials help students interpret the issues in summative feedback for their formative development, encouraging students to develop their work to achieve 'academic literacy,' writing in the way required by their discipline. Central to this process are exemplars that enable students to 'see' what is required. For example, the opportunity to see how another student has analysed evidence in an essay extract enables a student to see what is required in a concrete way that is not possible from the specification of criteria.

This foundation ensures that students take ownership of their work, by booking tutorials with tutors to discuss comments so they can align their work against the learning outcomes.

Activity: Recording a feedback tutorial

Copy the form for the Feedback Tutorial, p. 145 amend it for your purposes, and use it for a tutorial. Advice on implementation can be found in Case Study 8.

Learner Action Plan

The third stage of the Using Feedback Effectively strategy focuses on the development of a Learner Action Plan. Requiring students to develop a Learner

Action Plan recognizes that the developments in light of feedback will not happen unless specific and directed action is taken. A student user of the form noted: 'I realise that in order to develop my study skills I have to make an effort. I need to research these topics in the same way I do other aspects of my work' (in Burke 2007a).

Stephani (1998: 348) noted that staff assume that students know how to complete the tasks they are set, and 'rarely guide students through or model the process of structuring an essay'. Sommers (1982) also advised that tutors need to offer strategies for development so that students are not left playing a guessing game when it comes to acting on feedback advice.

One way to develop a plan is to start by identifying the major and minor points in tutor feedback. This opportunity to break feedback down into major and minor points is important, as they may be mixed up in tutor feedback, as illustrated by Sommers (1982: 151): 'Check your commas and semi-colons and think more about what you are thinking about'. Only by working out major and minor concerns will students be in a position to prioritize their efforts or work out a sequence for development.

Activity: Learner Action Plan Stage 1

Invite students to complete the Learner Action Plan Stage 1 to follow up issues in feedback.

Major issues	Minor errors
e.g. more analysis	e.g. Punctuation
1.	1.
2.	2.
3.	3.

Once students have decided what to work on, they can turn their attention to how to make the development. In most cases students will need to access some information, discuss an issue or develop a skill. Thus, it is useful to chart this process of development by identifying key resources in terms of people, books and online resources to assist their development in identified areas.

Activity: Learner Action Plan Stage 2

Invite students to complete the Learner Action Plan Stage 2 to follow up issues in feedback.

Issue	Tutor advice	Action to be taken
e.g. Referencing	To provide for citations, quotes and in bibliography	http://asp.wlv.ac.uk/ Level5.asp?UserType=6&Level5=500 Try out the advice for references in the essay. Book session with Study Skills Advisor to check if you have got it right.

You can add details to this section of the Using Feedback Effectively form to direct students to relevant study skills resources (people, book and electronic) which students can use in their action plan. Many tutors are sceptical about the benefit of reminding students about resources they have been informed about many times in the past. However, in the past such information might not have been relevant for the student if they did not know that they needed to develop in that area. This reminder of support at the point students need to access it makes it more likely that students will follow up advice. For example, if students have not referenced appropriately and do not take steps to learn how to reference, they will not be able to fulfil this aspect of academic work in future assignments. This form can be used as part of the feedback process to identify areas for the student to work on, together with details of a follow-up website or book.

It is important for all students to work out what they need to do to take their work to the next level (this is as important for students who want to move from B to A grades as for those who want to move from fail to pass grades). Often good students are frustrated by feedback which recognizes good achievement but does not offer advice for further development. They may need to cross-refer the feedback they receive to the marking criteria and examine the characteristics of the higher grade. This final stage aims to ensure that engaging with feedback becomes a learning experience for students, benefiting from the advice provided by tutors.

Acting on feedback: suggestions

1 Feedforward forms

Students can monitor their development through a feedforward process in which they add details to a feedforward box on the assignment feedback template or rubric. Here the student would indicate how they have attempted to follow up previous feedback and seek particular feedback on the success of their efforts. This brings to light the student quest to work on a particular aspect of their academic performance and seek external scrutiny for their efforts (see Case Study 5, pp. 135–7).

2 Recursive feedback

Case study 3 (pp. 130–1) reports on the process of recursive feedback used in a first year module. Students receive feedback on their essay that indicates areas for development which students have the opportunity to address. The feedback is very specific and certain sections of the essay are marked for change. Students also have a tutorial in which they can check their understanding of the feedback and the nature of the changes required. Students then resubmit their work and in reassessment only the marked sections are remarked, with the possibility of improving their overall mark for the essay by a grade band.

Resubmission provides students with an opportunity to complete the 'feedback loop'. Boud and Falchikov (2007: 185) advise that students are given the opportunity to respond to feedback. They recommend 'the testing of what has been learned through resort to evidence'. Taras (2006) develops this point further in relation to academic practice; she notes the exclusion of students from the normal iterative process within academia. Thus, while tutors benefit from an iterative cycle in the production of their work, students are expected to get things right first time. She states: 'Students are usually denied, by the same academics who benefit from expert iterative feedback, the possibility to update and improve their assignments by redrafting the work subsequent to tutor feedback' (2006: 366).

3 Reflection on skills development

Case study 4, pp. 132–4 reports on an exercise undertaken by students where they reflected on the process of resubmission within a skills module. Students were able to select a marked assignment for development and resubmission. They were required to maintain a reflective log to show the steps they followed to unpack the original feedback, and to detail the actions taken to address the feedback. This reflection enabled students to achieve closure by implementing the advice offered in feedback.

Summary

Getting more out of feedback can enhance the learning development of all students. Each assessment opportunity can become an opportunity for growth if we guide students to develop their own capacity to interpret and act on our feedback. The following comment reveals a student's changed attitude to feedback: 'Next time I complete an assignment, I am certain I will be more conscientious not to make the same mistakes but more importantly, remember my strengths too' (in Burke 2007a).

The Using Feedback Effectively strategy guides students through a range of processes to understand and use feedback, thus making them act on research findings that feedback should become central to their learning (Orrell 2006; Weaver 2006). It also responds to Orrell's (2006) research that while students may make a mental note of comments, most fail to follow the intention through.

The processes address many of the difficulties students may face in acting on feedback. It provides an opportunity to discuss seeming contradictions in feedback, and through discussion to overcome the tendency we have as tutors to make bland comments that do not recognize the level of challenges facing students. Clarity can be achieved through a tutorial, enabling the student and tutor to discuss the meaning and overall import of each comment, and ways to address the comments. This form encourages students to draw on a wide range of resources to aid their development, and provides links to people, books and electronic materials for support.

The encouraging statistic that 69 per cent of students enter higher education with the perception that feedback had helped their learning in the past means that students start with largely positive views of feedback. This strategy facilitates student understanding of feedback and supports their actions in relation to feedback. Please take the form and adapt it to your own situation so students can get more out of the feedback they receive (see Appendix, p. 149).

Recommended follow-up reading

Higgins, R., Hartley, P. and Skelton, A. (2001) Getting the message across: the problem of communicating assessment feedback. *Teaching in Higher Education*, 6 (2): 269–74.

Stephani, L.A. (1998) Assessment in partnership with learners. *Assessment and Evaluation in Higher Education*, 23(4): 339–50.

8

Feedback and personal development planning
Feeding forward

This chapter explores the contributions that staff from a range of university/ college departments can make to the process of students unpacking and acting on tutor feedback on their work. It explores the contribution that consultations and discussions outside the subject can make to student use of feedback: how peers can increase student understanding of tutor feedback; the role of skills tutors as a midway stage between peers and subject tutors; the role of learning development experts in addressing learning needs of individual students; plus the specialist inputs of library and information staff and university counsellors.

In an earlier chapter strategies for subject tutors to use with their students on marked work were explored. This chapter can be used by subject tutors to explore the range of support available to students outside of subjects. In addition the chapter is specifically relevant for staff involved in skills and student support, to explore their input into helping students act on subject tutor feedback.

Feedback and personal development • Support for student learning • Peer support • Skills tutors: expertise in writing and assignment skills • Personal tutors • University counsellors • Library information staff • Recommended follow-up reading

The feedback students receive on their work provides valuable information about the development of subject academic literacies. This feedback is necessarily complex and many higher education institutions (HEIs) offer a range of opportunities for students to discuss such feedback in the context of their personal development. This move outside subjects can help students reflect on their 'meta-cognition'; how feedback on assignments feeds into their understanding of their general performance, rather than the feedback being understood only in relation to the particular assignment. These opportunities to explore feedback can also help students develop their confidence and general academic skills.

Gibbs and Simpson (2004) drew on research from Brookhart which noted that successful students use feedback for self-assessment, seeking to learn from the feedback and for it to feedforward for future study. Teaching students to monitor their own performance is, in Sadler's (1989) theoretical analysis of the role of feedback, the ultimate goal of feedback. Students are likely to need to be taught how to use feedback to develop meta-cognitive control. Biggs (2003) identified metacognitive skills as the highest skill level, building on generic skills and study skills. Metacognitive skills involve the application of generic and study skills in new contexts.

This chapter has specific relevance for skills tutors and learning development staff but will also be useful in informing subject tutors of the assistance that students can get from other staff in following up feedback on their work. In light of such information subject tutors can make students aware of the different roles that staff across the institution can play for them in unpacking and acting on tutor feedback.

The UK Professional Standards Framework recognizes the valuable inputs of staff in both teaching and/or supporting student learning. Institutions are required to develop frameworks for student support and guidance. Figure 8.1 provides an example of one institution's 'road map' to inform students and staff about routes to support skills for learning.

Planning Skills tutor Module tutor	Grammar Skills tutor e-tutor	Stress Academic counsellor Peers
Referencing Subject librarian Module tutor	Who to contact to get more out of tutor feedback?	How am I doing? Personal tutor Module tutor
Subject resources Subject librarian Module tutor	Unpacking feedback Skills tutor Module tutor	Analysis Skills tutor Module tutor

FIGURE 8.1 One institution's 'road map' for routes to support.

Feedback and personal development

The view held by many students that feedback on a task is specific to that task and has no relevance to any other learning, has been identified by many as a major obstacle to students acting on feedback (e.g. Duncan et al. 2004). Such students hold a literal understanding of the term feedback, as backward looking comments on what they have achieved in past assessments. To uncap the formative potential of such comments, even on summative assessments, it is necessary to develop a new understanding of tutor 'feedback' which is freed from its retrospective spatial location. This makes it possible for tutor comments to inform students on their present and future learning by feeding forward and continuing to shape the student learning journey. Box 8.1 provides a reminder of the ASK approach which underpins these approaches to using feedback.

Box 8.1 The ASK approach to affecting change

This includes:
- ATTITUDE: Non-collection of assignments seems endemic across HE and proves to be the first hurdle in students' ability to act on feedback. We need to help students rethink their belief in assignment/learning closure (the assignment/module is finished and so there's no need to collect, make sense of and act on feedback since it has no connection with or relevance to future assignments/modules). Build into module design the need to receive and act on feedback, and ensure students are rewarded for doing so.
- STRATEGIES (recognition of variety of learning styles and needs as a starting point):
  - electronic links
  - academic study skills feedback tutorials (formative and summative)
  - e-tutoring
  - self- and peer-assessment
  - learning materials and resources
  - subject feedback tutorials (formative and summative)
  - workshops (skills and developmental)
- KNOWLEDGE (cognitive and practical): Understanding the need to act on feedback. Knowing how to act on feedback. Knowing that the development of skills is a personal investment of time. Acting – taking practical steps beyond merely acknowledging the need to or intentions to.

Most institutions now resource a wide range of pedagogical sections to facilitate student development. In the past the tendency in higher education was to regard such sections as remedial, to help those students who had not yet achieved the required standard. However, today the scenario has changed and most staff in HEIs note the need for all constituencies of students, traditional and non-traditional, to develop their skills during a degree course. This is due to changes in the nature of the student body and also changes to subject content. First, widening participation initiatives have been successful in extending the range of students entering higher education. The student body is very diverse and many new students start with a wide range of skills that may not fit the skills required on their course. Second, the changing curriculum in higher education requires students to develop a wide range of skills, and any one individual member of staff is unlikely to be able to support such a diverse range.

Activity: Starting points – what skills are required?

What learning skills were required for your degree course?
How do these compare with the skills required by students today?

For example, when I think back to my degree course in the 1970s I note that the range of skills required was quite limited. I had to take notes in lectures, contribute to seminars, research essays by finding books in the library and handwrite my essays. This meant that these skills were honed by constant consolidation. Dare I list the skills that were not required: keyboard skills, information literacy skills, presentations, working with others and work placements?

Staffing in higher education institutions now reflects this broader skills agenda and there is recognition that subject lecturers may not be the best suited to support the development of skills. Learning support is recognized as a profession and it is worth pausing to consider the ways that student learning is supported by such professional input.

The traditional view of feedback would be similar to the five functions of feedback proposed by Butler and Winne (1995). Feedback functions to engage with the conceptual and theoretical issues in the content of the student's essay, and the ability of students to provide appropriate information to display their understanding of key concepts. Thus, feedback is specifically related to subject academic understanding and application. Students are best advised to discuss such feedback with their subject tutor. However, other categorizations of feedback note the range of generic issues found in tutor feedback that go beyond such subject-specific engagement.

Hyatt (2005), for instance, identified seven categories within feedback. Central to these were subject-related topics on content, method and development. However, the majority of comments (and even aspects of method and development) concerned generic issues, namely phatic (developing a rapport with the student), structure, stylistic and administrative (see Table 8.1).

Table 8.1 Support for feedback categories between subject and skills tutors

Categorization	Subject tutor	Skills tutor
Butler and Winne (1995: 246)	1 conceptual understandings or beliefs 2 if lacking information 3 where elements of prior knowledge are inappropriate 4 help to tune understandings, discriminating between concepts 5 if holding false theories, need to restructure schemata	
Hyatt	phatic, content, method development	phatic, structure, stylistic administrative

Support for student learning

There are clearly some aspects of feedback that only the tutor who provided it can explore with the student, particularly in relation to subject understanding and ways of writing within the particular discipline. However, this specific subject-related feedback sits alongside more general feedback on academic skills in writing and information literacy. In these areas students can successfully be supported by skills tutors.

There are two main reasons why students may seek to discuss feedback with someone other than the subject tutor who provided the feedback. The first is a practical reason linked to very large numbers in some modules, which means that one tutor meeting with individual students is not feasible. Read et al. (2003, cited in Cramp, 2008: 211) state, 'constraints on lecturers' time and availability and large student numbers led to a conception of "distance" between lecturer and student'. This may mean it is easier for students to book a tutorial with a skills tutor than their subject tutor.

The second reason for a skills tutorial is not a second best option, but a different option for students who need to work on generic skills. We have noted the importance of dialogue to help students unpack tutor feedback, and in some cases this unpacking is best done away from the provider of the feedback. Some students may not want to discuss feedback that they perceive to be negative with the person who provided it, and the emotional aspect of receiving criticism may lead students to avoid a person who provided it.

In exploring tutor feedback students need to access the person/role most appropriate to their need at that time. Thus, a student may consult a range of staff during their learning journey. The following sections will explore the potential of a range of staff roles.

Starting with my own institution (University of Wolverhampton) as an example, students can discuss the feedback on their work with a range of academic and support staff. Within my own school, students can book one-to-one sessions with Academic tutors who have a role in skills development. They can also book an appointment with a skills tutor, many of whom are recent graduates who possess a degree in writing. In addition, new initiatives involve the provision of e-tutors to provide distance support.

Peer support

Moore et al. (2010: 33) in a section on 'peer supported learning' note that 'Experienced students tend to be closer from the points of view of time, culture and perspective to novice students, yet they have also learned some of the important rules, routines and skills of academia.' This recognition is important for tutors to consider in reflecting on ways that peers can support learning from feedback in their subjects. The situation may differ from subject to subject, depending on the nature of the learning challenge and the feasibility of students providing peer support.

Peer support is available in many institutions in formal or informal ways. Peer support can help students work out what the tutor comments mean, as the student who has received the feedback may feel more comfortable to ask questions about the feedback with a fellow student than a member of university staff. They may not want to ask questions that may be regarded as 'silly' or 'inappropriate' such as 'What does unconsolidated argument mean?' If the peers are friends, there may be closeness that allows for the asking of such questions, without the fear of losing face.

Students within the same module

Peers who are studying the same module have shared learning experiences and may be able to offer important support as they are following a similar learning journey. Cooper (2000: 290) drew attention to the benefit of peer reading, which is essentially a two-way process in which both parties benefit from the exercise. The reader develops critical skills in discerning academic criteria and making judgements about subject content, and the recipient gains in receiving non-threatening feedback on their work. This process of peer reading, Cooper stressed: 'refocuses students from what they *"do"* to pass an assignment, to the way they *think* about their work' (p.290, original emphasis).

Peers can also share a 'like experience' in coping with feedback that may seem negative, or be so vague that they work together to work out what tutor shorthand may mean.

There are also advantages to be gained in discussing tutor feedback on particular tasks, where students may be able to share things that each has received positive feedback on. This act of discussing and recognizing aspects can lead to a better understanding of what the task required, and thus an awareness of what to remember for the future. In addition, students benefit from the opportunities to share good practice and learn from each other. The student who is sharing also gains in personal confidence through the sharing of the recognition of success in tutor feedback comments.

Activity: Peer discussion of feedback

Get students to discuss their feedback with each other, to identify one thing they did well and share it with their partner.

They should then identify one thing they need to develop, and discuss with their partner how they might develop the necessary skills.

Peer mentors

Discussion with peers outside students' cohort, perhaps students from other years who they do not know, can offer a non-threatening opportunity to discuss feedback with someone they can ask questions of. This support may be both practical and psychological. On a practical level, such students are familiar with the feedback regime within the subject, and also know something about the subject content. They may be able to flesh out how they approached a similar assignment, sharing key sources of information or opening up discussion about key theories. On a psychological level, this input, from students who have successfully progressed to the next level, may provide an insider voice that is easier to listen to – easier as students can have some confidence that this peer voice is worth listening to because this person has 'been there and got the T shirt', so to speak. The form of expression used by peers may explain points in an easy to understand manner. Also peers are more likely to share an awareness of the challenges of learning that they may feel tutors do not recognize.

There is also an advantage to be gained from discussion of 'general' issues in feedback with students outside their subject. Mentoring programmes in many universities help 'peer mentors' develop skills in discussing work, asking questions and helping students interrogate their own work. Student Union input can provide skills workshops and support that helps students develop skills to degree level. The interactive and fun approach in peer-run sessions can help students tackle a learning issue in often novel and pressure-free ways.

Skills tutors: expertise in writing and assignment skills

Skills tutors are the main source of support for students. They operate in a range of different locations, within schools or learning centres. We use the term 'skills tutor' to cover the role of staff outside subjects who support the development of study skills (also known as study skills advisor, academic skills tutor, etc.). One of the creative developments at the University of Wolverhampton has been the development of the role of skills tutors within the Learning Centres. For the most part skills tutors are postgraduate students, who have a part-time contract to provide skills support. This means that many skills tutors stand midway between subject tutors and students, and they can play an important function in helping students understand tutor feedback. They may be regarded as more approachable as they are likely to be closer in age to students and in dealing with generic skills issues use language that students find easier to understand. The generalist approach during skills tutorials may mean that the focus of discussion about the feedback on essays is more understandable than discussion with subject tutors, where skills may be linked to complex subject concepts. There is also the issue that tutors may have forgotten what it is like to be a learner, whereas because many skills tutors are postgraduate students, they are still submitting work and receiving feedback on it. Such skills tutors are also likely to recognize that students may have difficulties interpreting feedback, while the tutor who provided the feedback may think that their comments are self-explanatory.

An additional and important point is that skills tutors are not involved in the assessment of student work so there is no fear of losing credibility with their subject tutor by asking questions. Students may feel they will not lose face by seeking support, as they may never see the skills tutor again, so it is an anonymous type of encounter. More importantly, skills tutors are not involved in marking student work, so there is no danger of students thinking that their marks may suffer in the future if they admit to the need to develop their work.

In relation to skills development, it is likely that skills tutors will have a greater knowledge of skills support materials than subject tutors. The focus of skills tutors' work on skills development means that they may be better able to direct students to support materials than subject tutors. Skills tutors bring an expertise in learning skills that subject tutors may not possess. Their focus on general academic skills means they are often in the best position to advise students on how to develop particular skills in writing and argument. They are also likely to have a greater familiarity with the research on the learning challenges students may face in writing and presenting their understanding in different assignment forms. Specific training and updating for their role are likely to cover relevant resources to support student learning. Discussion with other skills tutors is likely to lead to a sharing of experiences of working with students and a sharing of resources that students found useful.

In many institutions specific input from academic skills experts who have a background in adult literacy takes such skills inputs to a higher level. The recognition of particular challenges faced by adult learners can ensure that follow-up materials are appropriate for an adult rather than a younger learner. Skills tutors and writing departments in many universities have produced a range of electronic materials to support student learning. Such provision of pedagogically sound materials for adult learners, can offer tutorials to explore aspects of academic writing, and provide exemplars of real essays with tutor comments. Examples can be seen in many of the case studies.

E-tutors

A development of the skills tutor role has been the provision of e-tutors, initially within specific modules but now extended to whole cohorts. This role enables students who may not be able to attend tutorials, or who may lack the confidence to attend, to open up dialogue on their work in relation to academic skills. For the most part e-tutors provide support to students who are in the process of assignment writing, but in post-assessment periods, students are recommended to use the service to unpack and explore tutor feedback on their work. For an example of how e-tutoring works, look at the first case study in Chapter 9, pp. 125–7.

Personal tutors

Rounding off this chapter is a return to academic input provided through personal tutors. In most institutions personal tutors are members of academic staff who have a pastoral and developmental role for students who are study-ing their subject. Personal tutors are thus ideally suited to help students unpack and explore the feedback they have received across modules. Personal tutors are involved in the development of assessment and marking criteria within their subject, and they can use such experiences to help students understand the meaning and implications of feedback comments.

Discussion about feedback patterns within personal tutor sessions sends an important message to students that feedback is central to their development. It also addresses the issue raised by Cramp (2008: 212): 'Feedback comes in a variety of formats and types. How do level 1 students make sense of it?' Cramp provides examples of the ways that personal tutor tutorials help students to unpack feedback:

> Unpacking feedback: 'Written feedback is difficult to understand – much clearer when the personal tutor reads it out loud and showed how what looked like different comments may actually mean similar things.'

Synoptic reading to identify patterns: 'Helpful to look at assignments all together – reading feedback at different times meant that patterns weren't clear.'

(in Cramp 2008: 216)

At the University of Wolverhampton, all students are allocated to a personal tutor group, and periodically students are required to bring a summary of the feedback they have received on their work. This summary is used in the session to discuss ways forward and develop an action plan. This formal process can provide important support to students who may be struggling with the transition to higher education, and ensures that summative feedback is turned into formative guidance for the next semester.

University counsellors

Counsellors may offer the most appropriate support for students who are challenged by emotional issues in feedback. Counsellors are likely to be more aware of fragile student emotional states than other members of staff. Their expertise in helping students talk through emotional issues can help students who struggle to cope with negative feedback. In some instances they may be able to assist students to see that the feedback is not really negative, while in others they may be able to help individuals recognize that a major learning development is required to meet academic standards. This recognition may be difficult for students, and talking it through with a counsellor can help students take it on board.

In addition, counsellors may be able to help students develop skills in coping with stress and developing self-confidence. The wider issues of self-esteem and confidence are crucial for students to be able to recognize learning challenges and be confident enough to tackle those challenges.

Library information staff

In today's digital age library information staff (LIS) play an active role in student learning. Many universities look to LIS to keep abreast of the complexities of electronic information retrieval and referencing: 'Information literacy is knowing when and why you need information, where to find it, and how to evaluate, use and communicate it in an ethical manner' (CILIP 2004). This challenge is relevant to students acting on tutor feedback in relation to access to relevant source materials and appropriate referencing. In relation to sources,

LIS can assist students develop the skills they need to use databases and electronic search engines to access suitable materials. This assistance can also address issues in student use of sources. Bastable et al. (2008) reported on how students were able to gain a better understanding of the techniques to access relevant materials. In addition, the development of discriminatory skills and sound referencing were crucial in helping students avoid involuntary plagiarism.

Recommended follow-up reading

Boud, D. and Falchikov, N. (eds) (2007) *Rethinking Assessment in Higher Education: Learning for the Longer Term*. Abingdon: Routledge.

Cramp, A. (2008) Developing student engagement with, and reflection on, feedback through the tutorial system, in A. Wheeler (ed.) *Learning and Teaching Projects 2005–2007: Enhancing the Student Experience*. Wolverhampton: Institute for Learning Enhancement, pp. 211–20.

9

Case studies

This chapter fleshes out some of the initiatives set out in earlier chapters. These examples of the ways that feedback practices have been developed within subject disciplines allow you to consider how such approaches could be used or adapted to fit your purposes. In addition to case studies from our own practice, we include interesting examples from other subjects and institutions.

Each case study follows the same format (with some minor variation in Case Study 2):

Context This provides details of the subject and/or module in which the innovation was developed. This detail links to the specific learning outcomes of the module and demonstrates how the feedback adaptation better enabled students to achieve the outcomes.

Theoretical underpinning All innovations are linked to a theoretical understanding of the importance of student engagement with feedback to develop their learning.

Application This rich description fleshes out the application of the innovation to allow you to see the nature of the innovation, how it worked in practice and feedback from students.

Benefits and challenges This section weighs up the contribution that the case makes to student learning and tutor provision of feedback. Such benefits are set alongside the challenges that need to be addressed in implementing the case study.

Case Study 1. Dialogue in e-tutoring

This case study explores the way that students' academic competency can be enhanced through the use of frequent feedback on multiple drafts of a discipline-specific essay. It is of particular interest to tutors who would like to incorporate more formative learning activities but are deterred by large classes.

Context

First year students in an over-subscribed discipline-linked writing skills module engaged in dialogic feedback with writing e-tutors. Students composed a series of scaffolded drafts for a discipline-specific core module they were studying. Each draft was then submitted to an e-tutor for feedback that informed students on the next draft. This case study reveals that students benefit from receiving feedback on drafts because they can then *apply* that feedback and learn from the process of doing so.

Theoretical underpinning

Composition research indicates that for students to become better writers, they need timely and frequent feedback. The strategy of giving feedback on drafts and allowing students to *apply* their learning to the same or later assignment thus has great potential to enhance student engagement and development. In particular, students need *more* guidance during their first semester at university to help them understand what feedback *is*, and how they can use it. This initiative can be seen as a way of enabling students to become what Lave and Wenger (1991) would call 'legitimate peripheral members' of the academic community of a university. This innovation transforms feedback into feedforward through cumulative coursework, which entails building into the feedback process a more immediate opportunity for the student to make use of the feedback than would otherwise be the case in large classes (Hounsell 2007: 6–7). The form this typically takes is the cyclical one of draft-comment-revise-resubmit, mirroring the long-established strategy followed in composition and creative writing classrooms. It makes use of Brannon and Knoblauch's (1982) idea of the two-columned text presented in Chapter 3 as a way of engaging students in a dialogue that improves both their writing skills and promotes self-regulated learning.

Application

It is impossible for one lecturer to read and respond to over 150 texts on a weekly basis, so writing e-tutors were recruited and trained from a third year creative writing module to provide individualized feedback. Each first year student was assigned to one e-tutor according to the subject they were studying, so that e-tutors could help them to develop their discipline-specific writing skills.

Throughout the semester, first year students in the writing skills module produced a series of three essay-specific drafts for one of their discipline-specific core modules. They were required to send all three drafts to e-tutors via email as part of the writing module's portfolio assessment. Both students and e-tutors were expected to engage in email exchanges that enacted a dialogue about how to develop the drafts into a final polished essay.

The first draft, completed in week 4, required students to compose a double entry journal for examining the sources they intended to use for their polished essay. The left column of the journal summarized and quoted information from three scholarly articles or book chapters. The right column included students' responses to the sources, which could be about how the sources approached the topic or the validity of the findings or how the information might be used to support their answer to the essay question. Students sent the double-entry journal to e-tutors, who responded to the student's comments in the right column in an attempt to encourage more critical thinking and provide advice about how to use the sources effectively or about discipline-specific conventions for appropriate citation of sources.

Feedback from e-tutors was then used by students to generate a second draft, which was a five-paragraph essay that incorporated the sources examined in the double entry journal. Students were asked to compose the five-paragraph draft in two halves so that the left column contained the draft text and the right column provided their comments about each paragraph. Student comments could include statements about intention (what they were trying to do), difficulties with organizing information or constructing meaning (how they were trying to do it), effectiveness of sources as supporting evidence, and/or questions they wanted e-tutors to address in feedback. Second drafts were then sent to e-tutors in week 6, who returned the drafts the following week with responses to students' comments about each paragraph and offered advice about where the student writer might find additional information to improve the next draft. Students were asked to send an email to the e-tutor that responded to feedback comments, explaining how they would use the information or proceed on the next draft prior to composing it. E-tutors could then provide writers with advice about their plans for polishing the essay and/or their composing processes.

The final draft of the essay was submitted to e-tutors in week 10. This was accompanied by a letter which outlined what the writer was trying to accomplish, how close the writer thinks they came to answering the essay question, any difficulties experienced in composing the draft and places in the text the writer believed were particularly effective. E-tutors used this accompanying letter to guide their reading of and response to the draft and to point out areas where the student's self-appraisal was astute or somewhat misguided. Student writers used the final e-tutor advice to inform final revisions to the essay prior to completing a self-assessment form using the criteria discussed early on in the writing skills module and then submitting it for assessment in their core module.

Benefits and challenges

Benefits

- Students engaging in feedback dialogue through cumulative coursework tended to receive higher grades in the core module they wrote the polished essay for than in their other modules.
- End-of-module feedback from students, e-tutors and subject staff suggests this approach to individualized formative feedback has improved students' overall engagement with the assessment task.
- First year students indicated that they highly value being able to contact the more experienced e-tutors about their assignment writing and other student-related issues (e.g. procedures for assignment submission and extensions, access to campus computers and student support services, how to use new software, etc.) and claimed that they would welcome the use of e-tutoring services in the future.
- The cumulative coursework approach reinforced the writing process, reducing the tendency to procrastinate or trying to 'write right the first time' and the use of feedback throughout the writing process tended to improve writing skills and confidence as well as promoting self-regulated learning for future improvement.
- E-tutors going on to teach in schools gained first-hand experience in providing effective feedback and showed improvement in their own writing skills.

Challenges

- Setting up a system of e-tutoring is initially very labour-intensive for the tutor and requires continual monitoring throughout the semester.
- Not all first year students will participate in feedback dialogues in a timely or useful way (e.g. some students 'bunched' submissions to e-tutors when they missed a draft deadline).
- There were some criticisms from e-tutors that providing formative feedback on weaker students' work was time-consuming and impacted on their own ability to meet assignment deadlines.

Further information

Pieterick, J. (2009) CIEL Briefing Paper on Developing Academic Literacies. University of Wolverhampton Institute for Learning Enhancement. http://www.wlv.ac.uk/default.aspx?page=18197 (accessed 20 May 2010).

Case Study 2. Bioscience: comparison of staff and student views

This summary of the report comparing first year student and staff views about feedback was included to highlight research on feedback within a science subject. However, the issues raised about these comparative perspectives will be of interest to all staff.

Context

First year student perceptions of feedback on the Biological Sciences degree at the University of Leicester. Students receive regular written feedback on their work by way of a redesigned feedback sheet, which provides specific 'feedforward' guidance. This study reports on a comparison of staff and student perceptions of aspects of feedback, including the quantity, timing, use and quality of comments.

Application

The research with staff and students found common agreement on the purpose of feedback to provide information for students, with prompts drawing from students the benefits from feedback which identified errors in their work.

Quantity of feedback

Although students were generally positive about the quantity of feedback they received, about a third felt that more detail could be provided in written feedback.

Timing of feedback

Responses identified a strong appreciation of the benefit of immediate feedback on practical tasks, together with a recognition of the overview that 'delayed feedback' provided on summative tasks.

Use of feedback

The team noted Weaver's finding of the need to guide students on how to use feedback, thus, guidance is to be incorporated into a 'Study and communications' module. Staff and students noted variability in the use of feedback, representing the range from full and extensive use of tutor feedback to reading only the grade. Motivation was a key area identified by students, if the grade was close to their expectations, they were more likely to read it. The key issue of 'feed-forward' was noted as an area for discussion, as although some students did feel they could feed comments forward, staff were not able to identify where this had actually taken place.

Quality of feedback

Quality started with basic issues of accessibility, students appreciating feedback they could read and understand. The next level concerned the content of comments, where students wanted sufficient detail to know what was right in the work and where the errors were. This meant that comments needed to contain enough detail for students to see how to improve in future work.

Staff agreed with the need for feedback comments to be balanced between the praise for strengths and negative criticism for errors. They appreciated the psychological benefit of starting with the strengths in a piece of work before moving on to the critical points.

Benefits and challenges

Benefits

- Research ensures that tutors and students are aware of the other's perspective and can respond accordingly.
- Research identified the actual areas of student dissatisfaction.
- Involving students in such an investigation shows that the subject is taking the concerns of students seriously.

Challenges

- for tutors to provide students with personalized feedback, that demonstrates consistency;
- to help students understand the purpose of feedback by preparing them for the feedback they will achieve so it is in line with their expectations;
- to help students better understand how they can use feedback to improve future learning.

Further information

Bevan, R., Badge, J., Cann, A., Willmott, C. and Scott, J. (2008) Seeing eye-to-eye? Staff and student views on feedback. *Bioscience Education*, 12(1) [online] url:http://www.bioscience.heacademy.ac.uk/journal/vol12/beej-12-1.aspx (accessed 4 August 2009).

Case Study 3. Recursive feedback

This case study explores an innovation assessment regime that provided students with the opportunity to act on formative feedback prior to summative assessment.

Context

This innovation was implemented in a core level one module in special needs and inclusion studies in the School of Education, University of Wolverhampton. The aim was to encourage retention by designing the module to provide students with the opportunity to act on formative feedback before a final summative submission. The framework ensured that students collected their assignment, engaged with tutor feedback and took action prior to final submission.

Theoretical underpinning

The innovation was influenced by research by colleagues who identified problems with non-collection of marked work (Winter and Dye 2004) and research with students which identified the need for more detailed feedback on how to improve work (Davies and Wrighton 2004). In addition, the Special Needs subject team had concluded that students required the opportunity to improve their work before the module ended (Duncan et al. 2004). These findings were supported by Lea and Street's (2000) criticisms of modularity, and Hyland's (2000) recommendation to engage students in a 'dialogic feedback process'. Finally, the linking of formative and summative tasks encouraged by Ecclestone's (1998) research was incorporated into the design of assessment.

Application

The engagement of students in a dialogic feedback process is considered by many academics to be good practice (Hyland 2000), and essential to addressing the important problem of students not understanding what the tutors mean by their feedback.

Thus, students submitted the essay in week 8, and it was marked and returned by email two weeks later. Students had to attend a compulsory tutorial the following week, in which they were required to demonstrate their engagement with, and understanding of, tutor feedback. These were followed by seminars to help students develop points raised in feedback, before the essay was submitted for summative assessment at the end of the semester.

The re-design of the module reduced the amount of time in delivery of information to allow additional sessions to focus on student learning requirements. Students were required to attend the tutorial discussion to demonstrate their understanding of the feedback on their essay and indicate their intentions in following up feedback. Feedback focused on up to three specific changes that students could make to their essay, for example: 'This is a sound assignment which merits a C10, if you address the issues about referencing in the highlighted sections, your resubmission could raise your grade to a B13.'

In the final summative assessment, students submitted the original text and feedback, with highlights to show the sections they had added or changed. This process meant that the summative marking focused only on such sections, decided on how many out of the three points available were allocated to the student resubmission and added these to the original grade. The overall tutor comment justified the final grade, for example: 'Your work on the highlighted sections shows that you have acted on feedback advice and provided additional supporting evidence for your argument concerning autistic pupils. For your additional work in addressing issues in feedback you have been awarded an additional two grade points to raise your grade to B12.'

Benefits and challenges

Benefits

- There was an improved student pass rate on the module.
- The majority of students took the opportunity to act on feedback, even though it was voluntary.
- In these resubmissions students were successfully able to demonstrate their understanding of the issues raised in tutor feedback, as indicated by an average 2.4 grade point increase (out of a possible 3 points).

Challenges

- There was criticism that the approach pandered to student 'grade-fixation'. The team considered recommendations to withhold grades (Taras 2003) but decided to build on student interest in their grade as the motivating factor to 'learn more to earn more'. While this is not the ideal situation, it was felt to be an appropriate step if it helped students to develop the skills and confidence to remain on their course.
- There was criticism that the approach attempts to provide students with a 'failsafe' approach to study. This could be criticized as a lowering of standards. However, such a supportive approach to assessment helps students to develop skills rather than lower standards.

Further information

Duncan, N., Prowse, S., Burke, D. and Hughes, J. (2007) '. . . do that and I'll raise your grade': innovative module design and recursive feedback. *Teaching in Higher Education*, 12(4): 437–45.

Case Study 4. Reflecting on acting on feedback

This case study explores a range of activities undertaken to help students develop the ability to act on tutor feedback. It informs both skills and subject tutors about the range of activities that students can use to unpack tutor feedback.

Context

The module Personal, Academic and Career Enhancement (PACE) was offered to first year students in the School of Humanities at the University of Wolverhampton.

Theoretical underpinning

The module aimed to provide students with an effective start to their university course, acting on Cottrell's recommendation that 'changes in the student body go hand in hand with the need for different kinds of teaching and with increased emphasis on skills development' (2001: 6). The module situated the development of skills for study within a model of personal development, which meets the Dearing Report's requirement for students to 'learn how to learn'. Students were encouraged to develop their independence as a learner through opportunities to analyse how they stood in relation to 'skills' required for study. Learning outcomes for the module included the ability to use feedback effectively by recording the necessary steps and re-writing a negotiated assignment.

The approach was based on the work of Biggs (2003) who identified metacognitive skills as a third level of skills, which goes beyond generic and study skills. Metacognitive skills are in essence involved with 'what a learner does in a new context' (2003: 94), and involve an awareness of the self as a learner. This links to Race's (2001) work on leading students to conscious competence, which involves the self-awareness to assess their own learning against specified outcomes. We want students to know why they achieved a particular grade for an assignment, to be aware of their strengths and weaknesses, and to set targets for their own development in relation to tutor feedback on an essay. The activity on resubmitting an assignment applies Butler and Winne's advice that positions 'feedback within a model of self-regulation that guides cognitive activities during which knowledge is accreted, tuned, and restructured' (1995: 246).

This opportunity to learn from the experience of assessment is important, especially if the experience is a negative one. Cannon (2002) recommended helping 'students to manage and learn from setbacks'. The approach in this module supported students who struggled with the demands of academic writing, by providing them with the time and resources to develop skills to support their progress. Students were able to 'learn by doing', to utilize feedback to further their understanding of a task through resubmission. Butler and Winne (1995) advised a review of temporal location of feedback, so that it was set within the process of learning rather than at the end. Taras provided strong arguments for students having the opportunity to re-submit assignments. She pointed out that this enables students to use tutor feedback and provides an opportunity for students to check 'if they have internalized and completely taken the feedback on board' (2001: 609).

Application

Students used the 'Feedback effectively' form to guide and record their interaction with tutor feedback. One student introduced his work on this section with the words 'So . . . now I have the feedback . . . what am I to do with it?' This form responds to this question by guiding students to enable them to make the most of tutor feedback. In this module students were required to have a 30-minute tutorial to discuss strategies for acting on the feedback with their tutor. Stephani noted that staff assume that students know how to complete the tasks they are set, and staff 'rarely guide students through or model the process of structuring an essay' (1998: 348).

For this task students were able to select an assignment from either of their subjects for the re-submission exercise. This was an attempt to make this exercise relevant and link the skills development to their subject learning. The majority of students took the opportunity to work on a Religious Studies assignment; in some cases this was an essay that they had failed and would need to re-submit at a later stage. Students had individual tutorials with the module leader as well as with the tutors who provided the feedback on the actual essay they were going to re-write. Students were assessed on their reflection on their learning, the development of their action plan, and how far the final essay had addressed the points raised in feedback.

Student comments in response to the question 'Does acting on feedback by re-writing an essay help your learning?' showed general agreement with the exercise although their comments stressed that they felt they already had too much work and would only undertake such a task if it was worth their while in terms of grades or credits. Those who agreed (37.5%) felt the task helped to 'show me whether I have learnt from my mistakes', and 'to know what to improve'. Those in between (18.75%) recognized the value of working on drafts of an essay and receiving feedback that they could act on: 'if I do a draft and get feedback on it, I can do better in the final essay'. Those who disagreed (31.25%) with the benefits of the task, felt that their work could improve if they received generic advice as they did not see the benefit of spending time going over the same ground.

Overall, students in the pilot study found the feedback exercise helped them to engage with tutor feedback and to use feedback to develop their learning. The strongest comment in recognition of this benefit came from this student:

'I realize that in order to develop my study skills I have to make an effort. I need to research these topics in the same way I do other aspects of my work.'

Benefits and challenges

Benefits

- Familiarizing students with a process to act on tutor feedback helps them develop good habits which they may draw on in future learning experiences.
- Students learn how to act on feedback, how to discuss feedback with their tutor and identify points for future development. One student reported on the acting on feedback exercise: 'This exercise was interesting and helpful to complete, since I misunderstood some feedback I received and if I did not complete this exercise, I would have continued doing what I was, which would have had a negative impact on my work.'
- Students gain an awareness of the range of supports available for their learning.

Challenges

- The actual tutor feedback that students had to work with was often too brief or too vague for students to act on.
- Many students lacked the motivation to work on the feedback. They felt they had completed that task and wanted to move on to the next challenge, and not re-visit earlier work.
- The difficultly of acting on advice was identified as a major problem by students. Many stated that they felt it was very easy for tutors to make bland comments about study skill changes, which do not recognize the level of the challenge facing the student. Many students stated that they needed to have the opportunity within modules to develop the skills required for assessment.
- A key ingredient of preparation was a clear statement of what was required, many students stating the benefit of seeing this. Thus exemplars, not just of model essays but actual essays with usual feedback, were beneficial in enabling students to see what they have to do.

The following comment reveals a student's changed attitude to feedback: 'Next time I complete an assignment, I am certain I will be more conscientious not to make the same mistakes but more importantly, remember my strengths too.'

Further information

Burke, D. (2007) Engaging students in personal development planning: profiles, skills development and acting on feedback. *Discourse: Learning and Teaching in Philosophical and Religious Studies*, 6(2): 107–42. (Available online at http://prs.heacademy.ac.uk/view.html/PrsDiscourseArticles/1)

Case Study 5. Feedback/feedforward proformas

This case study summarizes the development of a feedback form to identify feedback from feedforward information. This information could be transferred to other subjects.

Context

This innovation was implemented for undergraduate Religious Studies students and used across all years by all members of staff. The form was used for marking all essays and received favourable feedback from both students and the subject external examiner.

Theoretical underpinning

This approach was developed to help students differentiate between tutor comments that feed back on their marked work and tutor comments that provide feedforward information to inform future learning. Research has shown that students are often unable to transfer tutor feedback on work from one assignment to the next, or from one module to the next, or from one subject to another. Such an understanding of feedback means that students look backwards and interpret comments as located in the past. This view also means that students feel passive in relation to the feedback; their work was finished and they cannot do anything about it. Thus, many students think tutor comments would be useful if they were to do the same essay again, but as they cannot, then the comments are not relevant to future learning.

Students express frustration with feedback comments that identify mistakes or problems without indicating to them how to put things right. Separate feedforward comments can specify the steps students need to take to develop their skills or align their work with subject expectations.

Application

The two sections for feedforward were added to the feedback sheet for Religious Studies, first, to split comments on aspects of performance into feedback and feedforward. The distinction is also shown by the use of different font colours for each area (green for feedback, and blue for feedforward). The feedback comments refer to what the student has done in the essay, recognizing achievement and areas for improvement. Feedforward comments guide students on how to do something about the areas for improvement.

	Feedback	Feedforward
Structure	You showed a good level of engagement with the material, but your focus on the question could have been tighter.	Explore this link for advice on structuring an argument http://www.monash.edu.au/lls/llonline/writing/arts/english/2.2.xml

The second reason was to identify one area for development and to accompany this with space for the student to note their intentions on reading the feedback. The identification of one area to work on can help students who are confused by the detail in tutor feedback. This helps students to prioritize their efforts by drawing on the main area for improvement for them to work on. This identification of a starting point can also help when students take their feedback to a skills tutor.

Staff recommendation: main area for you to work on

Develop your analysis, by way of the tutorial on developing a conclusion, to make more of your efforts.

Finally, students have the opportunity to take control of their next step by recording their intentions. Many students report that when they read feedback they do intend to make changes in future assignments but generally fail to follow that intention through. Thus, this final box in recording the intention seeks to give the student control over what happens next, and even if students forget, they can revisit the feedback and see what they intended to do.

Student action: make a note of your intentions on reading this feedback

---

Benefits and challenges

Benefits

The approach:

- clearly distinguishes feedback on the marked work from feedforward;

- makes it easier for students to unpack tutor comments;
- records the student's intention at the time of their reading of the feedback, thus making it more likely that the student will take note of it.

Challenges

- Tutors face the challenge of dividing their comments between feedback and feedforward.
- Encouraging students to act on the feedforward advice is still an issue. The separation of feedback and feedforward may make it easier to see what is required to develop their skills.

Further information

Burke, D. (2009) *Linked Learning: Hyperlinks in Feedback Webfolio.* http:// pebblepad.wlv.ac.uk/webfolio.aspx?webfolioid=1112466) (accessed 30 June 2009).

Case Study 6. Hyperlinks in feedback

This case study sets out the inclusion of hyperlinks to support materials in tutor feedback. This approach can be transferred to other subjects as many of the hyperlinks were to generic skills material.

Context

Hyperlinks were used in a History module with 80 first year students. This module on the Holocaust was a popular elective option for students, and the first History module that many students had taken. Thus, many students needed to develop their historiographical skills in order to be successful in the exam at the end of the module.

Theoretical underpinning

In earlier studies with students (Burke 2009), research highlighted the fact that students often failed to follow up tutor feedback because they did not know what to do with it. One student commented: 'Now I've got the feedback, what do I do with it?' Stephani (1998) noted that students want information on how to develop their work. This case study addresses these points by providing links to sources that expand on feedback points and provide exemplars and online tutorials. It considers how study skills provision can be developed in light of Weaver's (2006) finding that only 4 per cent of students used study skills books for guidance on how to follow up feedback. The report demonstrates a way of building information and contacts into the actual feedback, by providing hyperlinks that take students directly to relevant sources. All students need to do is click the mouse to access material which will help them develop their subject learning or study skills.

Feedback banks have been identified as an important resource for tutors in providing access to the range of statements that tutors are likely to make on student work. In this instance the aim is to build on such work but to focus on statements that link to electronic resources for students to use in following up feedback advice.

The implementation of this electronic links strategy is based on the understanding that students are likely to follow up suggestions if it easy for them to do so. McGinty (2009) noted student attempts to follow up feedback by checking out academic conventions, even from study skills books, are far from straightforward. In this approach the suggestions can be followed up through hyperlinks which take students directly to relevant sources.

Walsh, in monitoring student 'needs' in the area of unpacking and using tutor feedback, noted that students in one-to-one sessions were very positive about the inclusion of links in feedback to electronic sources (Bartholomew and Walsh 2008). She found that students naturally use the Internet for research, so find it easier to use hyperlinks for follow up than to have to go to the learning centre and find recommended texts. In addition to the task of guiding students on how to act on tutor feedback, she found that students valued sites that addressed their particular needs as undergraduates in meeting the requirements of higher education.

Application

The implementation of the pilot on electronic links started with the identification of specific areas of study skill and subject application that students need to follow up, and the identification of electronic resources to meet these needs. Needs were identified through an examination of tutor feedback within two first year modules over the previous two years, noting advice on skill and subject development areas. Then a list was made of relevant study skills topics within our own 'Sharpen up Your Skills' website, with additional links to subject-specific resources in the Monash Writing website.

In addition, the strategy is designed to provide students with links to materials that meet their specific needs. Stephani noted that students want information on how to develop their work, and questioned the assumption held by many staff, that students know how to complete set tasks, which means that they 'rarely guide students through or model the process of structuring an essay' (1998: 348). This strategy addresses this point by providing links to sources that expand on feedback advice and provide exemplars and online tutorials. At this stage the links are to resources that already exist but the need to develop specific resources has been identified.

Initial student feedback on interactive tutorials and exemplars of student work has been very positive. This opportunity to compare their work with an exemplar can help students stand back from their own work and objectively consider their assignments. Thus, for example, looking again at their introduction after they have considered an example of a student essay with tutor annotations, enables them to analyse each against the requirements of an introduction. This process can help students 'see' what an essay looks like, with exemplars highlighting good writing. This exemplifies the advice from Chanock that students need to see 'a model of both process and product' and thereby be 'shown roughly what it might look like and how to put it together' (2000: 103). This process also addresses the weakness of approaches to essay writing, noted by Prosser and Webb, that 'students are not challenged to reflect on their own conceptions of what an essay is in the particular academic discipline' (1994: 136). They suggest that 'systematic' analysis of essays can help students develop an understanding of different approaches to writing, from which they can make adaptations in relation to the particular task and its context.

Benefits and challenges

Benefits

- This focus on what Hyatt termed the 'pedagogic role' of written feedback, can 'facilitate learning' by making it easy for students to follow up feedback advice, as well as playing 'an induction role into the academic discourse community' (Hyatt 2005: 351) through the provision of exemplars.
- This process can help to make transparent the 'academic conventions' that tutors may take for granted, and such exemplars allow students 'adequate participation' (Lillis and Turner 2001: 66).
- The use of subject-specific examples helped students 'see' how skills requirements for planning, structuring and referencing looked within their own discipline.

Challenges

- One of the main issues about hyperlinks is that the content of external sites may change and not remain relevant to the intended purpose.
- Provision of internal sites can be technically challenging, although the ability to develop materials that you put online reduces the reliance on others. The next case study explores webfolios, which in essence are individually controlled web pages that tutors can easily change or update.
- Dare I say it – we can provide the links but students still need to click on them to access the content!

Thus, the provision of hyperlinks to electronic resources offers a way to make tutor feedback more efficient by linking to materials that address individual student needs, and the ease of use encourages students to explore ways to act on the feedback.

Further information

Burke, D. (2008) Using electronic sources to help students get more out of tutor feedback. Paper presented at European First Year Experience Conference 2008, University of Wolverhampton, 8 May.

Burke, D. (2009) *Linked Learning: Hyperlinks in Feedback Webfolio.* http://pebblepad.wlv.ac.uk/webfolio.aspx?webfolioid=1112466) (accessed 30 June 2009).

Case Study 7. Linked webfolios

This is a short account of a recent development to use a webfolio that is linked to a module. These can be used by students while they undertake the assessment task. However, the main focus for this case study is the use of a webfolio page to close the feedback loop by providing examples of good practice.

Context

The aim was to create an easy way to provide students with examples of good practice at the time they received feedback on their work. Webfolios have been used within some Religious Studies modules so students are already familiar with their use for learning about content. This case study explores the use of webfolios for assessment purposes, to support student learning both during the completion of assignments and when they receive feedback. A webfolio is essentially a webpage that is easy for tutors to create and update. It can be sent directly to individual students or if published to the web, accessed via a url that is contained in the feedback form.

Theoretical underpinning

One of the key challenges facing students in higher education is learning to write according to the requirements of their discipline(s). However, it can be difficult to see how the subject discourse requirements would apply in the specific task set. Some students may think they have met these requirements and are unable to see the gap between where their work is and what is expected within the subject. To provide the student with an exemplar that is specific to the task undertaken can make it easier for the penny to drop and for a student to see a difference between their own work and work at a higher level. This opportunity to see work at a higher level can stimulate the student's cognitive development by showing them a standard they can aspire to. The exemplar is not only specific to their discipline, but also specific to the task they have received feedback on. The case study on hyperlinks identified the value of exemplars to aid student learning from feedback; webfolios take this process further as they enable staff to provide specific and relevant materials.

Application

The following box provides an example of exemplary material for students.

Consult the linked webfolio for initial guidance and illustrations of good practice: http://pebblepad.wlv.ac.uk/webfolio.aspx?webfolioid=966245

The url link to the webfolio is provided at the bottom of the feedback sheet for the task. Thus, all students need to do is click on the link to access the webfolio. The webfolio contains information to help students unpack and reflect on their feedback. One level of material reminds students of the academic requirements for referencing and provides examples of appropriate practice from the cohort. This allows students to see exactly how to reference texts they used for the task. The next level of material contains examples of student work, again from the task undertaken, with a commentary to draw attention to features of the extracts.

Thus, for example, an extract from an introduction was accompanied with this commentary: 'This page provides examples of actual student work for this assignment. The examples are from different students and should help you to think about your own work, and consider ways that you could make more of your research and understanding in future assignments.'

Introduction: *Look at this introduction; notice how the first example provides a succinct account of the issue under consideration for the task. Think about how you could improve this introduction, then look back at your own introduction and think how you could develop it to clearly state your intentions for the set assessed task.*

Example 1: 'In the past the world religion of Sikhism has experienced frustration in relation to how it has been portrayed and observed by academic sources. Many non-Sikh scholars, such as McLeod, have been condemned by members of the Sikh community for not showing what they believe to be an accurate picture of Sikhism. This essay explores this issue by considering textbook accounts of Khalsa Sikhs' observance in wearing the Kara bangle; this will then be matched against the primary source evidence, provided by Mr. Singh, a practising Khalsa Sikh and member of the teaching staff at the

> Guru Nanak Gurdwara in Wolverhampton. While any similarities between the different accounts shall be discussed, the main onus shall be on examining any differences. Further to this, two main reasons for the differences between academic text accounts and insider Sikh accounts will be explored.'

A second example has proved to be very popular with students. The extract shows them a good example of analysis within the task undertaken. In this instance students had to explain differences they had noted in the way Sikhism was presented by an insider source on a visit to the Gurdwara, and in the way Sikhism was presented in an outsider academic text book.

Analysis: in this section students are advised to look at the reasons provided in this account for the differences between the explanation provided during the field visit and the text book account.

Example 2: 'The issue of insider/outsider sources in the study of religion is a complex one and there are many reasons for inconsistencies between the two. Firstly, it must be understood that "many religions are far more diverse and heterodox than both insider and outsider accounts convey through written texts" (Chryssides and Geaves 2007: 238). This means that there may be no one authentic set of traditions within the stated religion, thus different accounts may be justified. Writing on this theme Smart (1989: 11) states that traditions "manifest themselves as a loosely held-together family of sub traditions." It would then be very impractical indeed for any author to observe every one of these sub-traditions and claim them as authentic to all adherents of the particular faith. What may be seen as authentic Sikhism to one particular assemblage of Sikhs may be very different to another, thus giving an outsider, wishing to write an accurate account of Sikhism, the problem of what, and what not to include in their particular narrative of the religion. Therefore many authors, including the three used here and identified as outsider sources, have presented only the most "prominent orthodoxies" (Chryssides and Geaves, 2007: 207).'

Benefits and challenges

Benefits

- The practicality of webfolios is their main advantage in allowing tutors to produce relevant materials for students to explore at the same time as they receive feedback on their work.
- Webfolios are easy for students to access, either via the url or by saving to the students' own assets.

Challenges

- Within Humanities subjects there are often no single right answers, thus all examples are subject to some qualification. In many cases this can be dealt with by providing students with a couple of examples, and with a commentary that encourages students to think about particular aspects of each example.
- Tutors face a technological challenge in putting the webfolio together. Packages available to tutors will depend on their institution. In most cases webfolios are likely to be linked to PDP policies that provide students with opportunities to put electronic portfolios together.

Further information

Burke, D. (2009) *Linked Learning: Hyperlinks in Feedback Webfolio.* http://pebblepad.wlv.ac.uk/webfolio.aspx?webfolioid=1112466) (accessed 30 June 2009).

Case Study 8. Feedback Tutorial Template: skills tutors

This case study explores the use of a template to support student tutorials with a skills tutor. The template could also be used by subject tutors to follow up feedback tutorials with students.

Context

Students can book one-to-one sessions with skills tutors through the learning centres or academic development centres in several schools within the university. Sessions last between twenty to forty minutes and students have been encouraged to use these opportunities to get more out of tutor feedback. Posters have advertised the opportunity to bring marked essays and the feedback to sessions so that academic writing issues raised in the feedback can be discussed with skills tutors.

The Feedback Tutorial Template has been developed, piloted and rolled out under the guidance of Wolverhampton University's Centre for Academic Skills. The purpose of the Centre is to develop and deliver academic skills across a broad portfolio of support provision within the School of Law, Social Sciences and Communications. This serves to enhance student progression and retention by supporting the development of academic literacies and academic socialization. The majority of the Centre's work occurs face to face with students in individual or group sessions. However, research to underpin such encounters is essential and since 2008 specific research has focused on the use of feedback tutorials.

Theoretical underpinning

The Feedback Tutorial Template on p. 145 provides a way of structuring such sessions so that a record of the discussion is provided and the student is offered a way of following up the issue flagged in tutor feedback. This approach engages with Nicol and Macfarlane-Dick's (2006a) sixth principle of good feedback by providing a practical opportunity for students to close the gap, indicated by feedback on their work, and move to the desired level of performance, as indicated by assessment criteria and illustrated by exemplars. Bartholomew and Walsh's research (2008) identified student views of the barriers to using feedback effectively, which may be clustered into three areas: translation; transferability and targets. The feedback tutorial addresses issues about the translation of feedback into language students can understand. Discussion with skills tutors can help students transfer academic feedback on one task to future learning in other modules. Students can be helped to see how to apply advice or recommendations from one tutor to their learning in other areas. This opportunity to extract guidance for future learning targets from feedback is one of the key benefits from a feedback tutorial. Skills tutors can help students turn academic comments into 'student-centred goals'. The challenge was to formalize this encounter so that students could be offered a summary of the discussion and guidance for future action.

Application

The Feedback Tutorial Template was designed to provide a means to summarize the session and to offer specific guidance for the future by way of hyperlinks to materials. The Word template allows a skills tutor to complete sections during the session and email the information to the student. The short time available for the tutorial meant that the template had to be easy to use. Thus, boxes at the top of the template record the question or feedback issue that the student raised during the tutorial. Following discussion, the skills tutor is then in a position to suggest follow-up materials to help the student develop in the area indicated from subject tutor feedback. Hyperlinks to materials are contained on the form, and can be selected and pasted into the 'follow up' box for the student to access. The form is then sent directly to the student by accessing the 'send to' 'mail recipient' option in the File option in Microsoft Word. The student receives an email summary of the tutorial and the hyperlink to relevant electronic sources.

A survey of issues raised by tutors in the School of Humanities (Bartholomew and Walsh 2008) identified the range of academic writing issues raised by staff, and charts providing materials which would help students address these issues were developed. In this process of development we noted that students needed different types of materials to meet their needs. Some students just needed to be reminded or informed of the characteristics of an aspect of academic writing.

Many students needed the opportunity to develop a particular skill, and thus required interactive materials allowing them to go through the process of developing and then checking their understanding of a skill. Online tutorials were identified as a good way of developing such skills.

In addition, because of the demand made by many students to 'see' what was required by tutors in their feedback, exemplars were identified as a good way for students to explore aspects of academic writing. This provision of examples enabled students to see why particular comments had been made about their work, and also to show them what would be a more appropriate presentation of material. For example, skills tutors in addressing tutor comments about the need to 'use' quotation, would be able to draw on an example where the student had drawn out the implications of the quote and applied them to the set task.

The student would then be able to consider their own practice and how they could apply this skill for their academic writing to be informed by scholarly works in the work they were discussing with the skills tutor.

The template makes it possible for a skills tutor to work within a short time-slot to explore one aspect of tutor feedback and offer some materials to start to address the feedback. The provision of hyperlinks has the advantage of any-time anyplace accessibility for students. Research by Cottrell (2001) identified the reluctance of students to consult study skills texts in following up tutor feedback, and hyperlinks make it easy for students to access information from the convenience of their own study. Hyperlinks can also take students directly to suggested materials, rather than leave them ploughing through sections of a book.

Feedback Tutorial *Example*

Summary of learning needs to be developed:

Your tutor noted that you demonstrated a good understanding of the general topic but that you needed to develop your planning so that you use the information to answer the set question.

– **specific feedback from tutor** – **identified from looking at work** – **response to student query**	*We looked at the tutor feedback and comments on the text of your essay to see where you could have used material more explicitly, and also at the importance of cutting out material that was not relevant.*

Hyperlinks: These links will take you to sources that will support your learning:

Try this tutorial on structuring an argument http://www.monash.edu.au/lls/llonline/writing/arts/english/2.2.xml

Benefits and challenges

Benefits

- The form has been used by a number of skills tutors who found the process easy to follow.
- The model guides a student's ability to *prioritize* problem areas. Students felt confident and motivated to use the hyperlinks identified by the tutor to directly access an appropriate resource: 'I start with one link and work across the three recommended areas.'
- The template has the flexibility to offer opportunities to improve which are appropriate to student *learning style*. Some links offer pure information, some offer opportunities to practise skills and others offer visual examples of quality work; students voiced satisfaction at this element of choice. One student, who enjoyed the interactivity of the quiz links, reflected that 'I learn best by testing myself.'
- The sheer *convenience* of e-access to resources was also a significant plus point within student feedback. Students expressed a greater willingness to explore an electronic link 'than to look at a study skills book'.
- Customization of the feedback to the *level and nature* of student need was the fourth area for comment. Some of the links are more complex than others and some are more practical. One student noted this link to her needs: 'I knew the theory, so the advisor just sent me a link to the practice site.'
- Others commented that the links were conducive to their preference for a 'little and often' small-step skill-building approach.

Challenges

- It would be preferable for links to be personalized to make them specific to the individual.
- This was also linked to the suggestion that students be provided with guidance about the actual steps for improvement.
- There was a suggestion that the role of exemplars should feed into the preparation for assignments, particularly the use of mid-standard exemplars, so students can explore strengths and weaknesses in relation to the task they are undertaking.
- Reservations were raised about the process if hyperlinks were provided without tutorial support, as it was generally recognized that the feedback links could not replace one-to-one feedback.
- Some of the participants were wary about recommending links without prior knowledge of the content.
- The level of engagement and commitment of the staff and students were also questioned, as were computer access and relevant IT skills of the students.

However, whatever our efforts, strategies, or other developments in feedback, we still face the same question: will students take any notice? Hyperlinks are not a magical solution to the problem; they will only work if students click on the link, read the materials and relate them to the issues raised by tutors in their feedback.

One reason why students do not act on tutor feedback is that it is difficult to do so. Part of the difficulty clearly lies in the feedback provided by tutors, but skilful reading by skills tutors can draw some learning for the student from most feedback. The difficulty addressed by this initiative is the problem of acting on the feedback. This provides both a strategy – the template – and practical materials – hyperlinks – to support student learning from feedback.

(A parallel strand to the Feedback Tutorial Template is a version for subject staff that encourages staff to provide hyperlinks to relevant materials in their feedback to students. Examples of this process can be seen in the linked webfolio for Religious Studies and History.)

Further information

Bartholomew, S., Burke, D. and Oldham, S. (2009) 'Feedback Tutorial Template: Links to learning.' Workshop, 3rd International Personal Tutoring and Academic Advising Conference: Improving student success. Liverpool, April.
Burke, D. (2009) *Linked Learning: Hyperlinks in Feedback Webfolio.* http://pebblepad.wlv.ac.uk/webfolio.aspx?webfolioid=1112466) (accessed 30 June 2009).

Case Study 9. Delivering oral and visual feedback online to students

Context

This case study summarizes McLaughlin's research at the University of Edinburgh with first year students. This pilot reports on the use of software which presents the student with screen shots with an audio commentary that explains the marking and provides suggestions for improvement.

Theoretical underpinning

This method was developed in light of research on learning styles, to provide feedback that would make more sense to students with visual, aural or kinesthetic learning styles. The decision to focus on end comments rather than a running commentary while marking was taken in light of student feedback that the summative comments were the most important to them. In addition, student feedback showed an appreciation of the way the video helped to personalize feedback.

Application

A system was developed to allow staff to produce a 'screen recording with simultaneous commentary'. Thus, tutors open the toolbar within Microsoft Word, to enter the comment function which was integrated with Camtasia software to allow screen recording while explaining comments on the essay script to students. This video feedback is provided at the end of the essay, at the time when a tutor usually provides summative comments on the whole work. Thus, the tutor focuses on what was good in the essay, pointing out why it was good, and identifies areas that would benefit from improvement, with suggestions provided to develop learning.

Benefits and challenges

Benefits

'I thought it was very useful, it made me look more critically at the essay and it helps considerably in seeing why the marker has given a certain mark and knowing exactly where you went wrong.'

- Students can access the feedback easily via a web link.
- Students are able to hear the tutor explanation for the comments on their work.
- Student feedback reports that the verbal commentary is more personal and deals with the issue of explaining the marker's comments.
- Student reported that the feedback was better than they expected, in particular because it addressed generic writing issues that they could work on for future essays.

Challenges

- More detail needs to be built in to the commentary.
- Staff need to be encouraged to develop the IT competence to engage with online materials.
- Students must be helped to appreciate that the commentary constituted feedback.

Further information

McLaughlin, P. (2008) *A System to Deliver Oral and Visual Feedback On-line, Personal to Each Student.* Centre for Bioscience, Higher Education Academy, York.
(http://www.bioscience.heacademy.ac.uk/ftp/DTES/mclaughlinwebrep.pdf) (accessed 20th November 2009).

Appendix

Using the Feedback Effectively form

The feedback you receive on your work is a good guide on how your work is progressing. The comments provide information on how far you have achieved the learning outcomes for the assignment, and comments on the text provide suggestions for improving aspects of your academic writing. Use this form to develop your skills in this area.

1 Working on feedback

Invite students to use this chart to break down your feedback using the following instructions:

Read the feedback on your assignment carefully, then re-read the piece of work to see the areas that the feedback refers to. You might use a highlighter pen to cross-refer the feedback to your work, or to draw attention to corrections and suggestions.

What has your tutor written?	What do you understand this to mean?
Break the feedback down into	
Good points *(note these down so you can do them again)*	**Areas for improvement** *(draw out the two main areas from feedback)*

2 Preparing for a tutorial

Use these prompts to prepare for a tutorial with your module tutor. Make an appointment with your tutor; take this form and your assignment to the tutorial.	
Feedback that you understand	**Fill in the actions you intend to take on these points and discuss with your tutor**
Feedback you do not understand	**Fill this column in during the tutorial**

Action Plan: Stage 1 *Divide the main feedback between:*	
Major issues	**Minor errors**
e.g. More analysis 1. 2. 3.	e.g. Punctuation 1. 2. 3.

Stage 2		
Issue	**Tutor advice**	**Action to be taken**
e.g. Referencing	To provide for citations, quotes and in bibliography	www.wlv.ac.uk/help Book session with Study Skills Advisor

Area to develop	Where to go for help
Study Skills: *if the advice is that you need to brush up on study or writing skills, you might find a section listed below will help.*	Moore, S., Neville, C., Murphy, M. and Connolly, C. (2010) *Ultimate Study Skills Handbook*. Maidenhead: McGraw-Hill, Open University Press.
Academic writing: *planning, developing an argument, grammar (sentence construction, punctuation, use of apostrophe), referencing.*	**Study Skills Advisors:**
Extend your reading base: *to find appropriate sources for your work: online catalogue (books and journals), electronic databases, the Internet.*	**Academic librarians:**
Coping with stress: *not able to focus on your work, worrying about failure, how to develop your confidence.*	**Counselling and guidance:** make an appointment at . . . **Student Union**

Example of institutional preparation

Induction Advice for all students: Getting more out of Tutor feedback on your work (University of Wolverhampton).

'OK I've got the feedback on my essay – what do I do with it?'
Academic writing at university, often within a new discipline, is a major challenge. Tutors have a role not just in presenting the subject, but also in helping you to align the skills you already possess to meet the challenges of academic writing. You may also find that assessment tasks require you to develop new skills, or adapt the skills you already possess. In these situations the feedback tutors provide on your work is particularly important.

Here are some suggestions on ways that you can get more out of tutor feedback . . .

Working systematically through feedback	
Often when you look at feedback it can all look negative (particularly if it is in colour!): pointing out spelling or grammatical mistakes, factual errors, questioning your interpretations and reminding you of the need to reference correctly. Taking negative points on board is very difficult so you may be inclined not to read the feedback. However, it is important that you read through the feedback carefully and make a note of all the things you can learn from it. This activity will help you to take a balanced view of your feedback, recording both the things you have done well and the areas for improvement.	**Areas for development** *Identify the things your tutor has noted that you need to develop, both comments on your assignment and on your feedback form.* **Good points** *Make a note of all the positive comments made by your tutor on things you have done well, so you know to continue to do them in future assignments.*
Preparing for a tutorial	
Check out arrangements for seeing your module tutor. You might want to book a specific tutorial time or just turn up when your tutor has office hours. Use the Using Feedback Effectively form to prepare by going through the feedback on your essay and filling in the chart.	**Work out the questions you want to ask your tutor before the tutorial:** Set out the feedback you understand and take the opportunity to check with your tutor that your understanding is correct. Other comments may seem vague so it is worth checking with your tutor how you could, for example, bring in 'more critical reflection'.

Making a Learner Action Plan	
This is the stage where you decide what to do about the feedback. Has your tutor indicated that there is something that you need to work on now which will improve your work in all areas for the future? For example, if you have not referenced appropriately and do not take steps to learn how to reference, you will not be able to fulfil this aspect of academic work in future assignments. Work out what you need to do to take your work to the next level (this is as important for students who want to move from B to A grades as for those who want to move from fail to pass grades).	**Major issues** 1.*Harvard referencing* **What are you going to do about it?** *I will use the guidance in Sharpen Up Your Skills* http://asp.wlv.ac.uk/Level5.asp?UserType=6&Level5=500 **Minor issues** 1.*Use of apostrophe* **What are you going to do about it?** *I will check out the link provided by my tutor:* http://humanities.ucsd.edu/writing/grammar/35apostrophe.htm
Locating appropriate follow-up	
There are a vast range of sources to support your development, below are some suggestions.	Click here for more information on 'Getting more out of tutor feedback' in the *Sharpen Up Your Skills website.*

Area for support	Where to look/who to contact
Study skills: if the advice is that you need to brush up on study or writing skills, these books and others in the study skills collections will help.	**Books:** Moore, S., Neville, C., Murphy, M. and Connolly, C. (2010) *The Ultimate Study Skills Handbook.* Maidenhead: McGraw-Hill, Open University Press.
Academic writing: planning, developing an argument, grammar and referencing.	**Study Skills Advisors:** learning centres Check if your school has specific skills support.
Extend your reading base: to find appropriate sources for your work: OPAC (books and journals), electronic sources, and how to use the Internet.	**Academic librarians:** there are help desks in all learning centres.
Coping with stress: not able to focus on your work, worrying about failure, how to develop your confidence.	**Counselling and guidance:** make an appointment. **Student Union:** Advice and Support Centre

Annotated Bibliography

Andrade, H. (2001) The effects of instructional rubrics on learning to write. *Current Issues in Education*, 4(4). <http://cie.ed.asu.edu/volume4/number4/> (accessed 15 August 2009).

Article examines the impact of instructional rubrics on students' writing and on their knowledge of the qualities of effective writing.

Ashwell, T. (2000) Patterns of teacher response to student writing in a multiple-draft composition classroom: is content feedback followed by form feedback the best method? *Journal of Second Language Writing*, 9(3): 227–57.

Study examined four different patterns of feedback provided to second language students that revealed students relied heavily on form feedback while content feedback had only a moderate effect on revision.

Askew, S. and Lodge, C. (2000) Gifts, ping-pongs and loops – linking feedback and learning, in S. Askew (ed.) *Feedback for Learning*. London: RoutledgeFalmer.

Useful article in a text edited by Askew. The co-constructivist approach to feedback is set out as a good approach to link feedback and learning.

Assessment Resource Centre (2005) *Constructing Assessment Criteria*. The Hong Kong Polytechnic University. <http://www.polyu.edu.hk/assessment/arc> (accessed 20 February 2009).

Provides practical advice about using assessment criteria to create proformas and rubrics.

Bangert-Drowns, R.L., Kulik, C.L, Kulik, J.A. and Morgan, M.T. (1991) The instructional effect of feedback in test-like events. *Review of Educational Research*, 61(2): 213–38.

Article examines feedback on tests and concludes that tutors can circumvent misinformation by providing feedback that points out erroneous thinking and supplies correct responses.

Bardine, B., Bardine, M. and Deegan, E. (2000) Beyond the red pen: clarifying our role in the response process. *English Journal*, 90(1): 94–101.

Article contends that written comments can become powerful teaching tools if supported by an individual teacher-student writing conference.

Bartholomew, S. Burke, D. and Oldham, S. (2009) Feedback tutorial template: links to learning. Workshop, 3rd International Personal Tutoring and Academic Advising Conference: Improving Student Success, Liverpool, 22 April.

Report on joint project from the perspective of academic tutor and support tutors, to chart the development of a feedback tutorial template to record and support student learning from tutor feedback.

Bartholomew, S. and Oldham, S. (2009) Feedback links in face to face and e-advice sessions. University of Wolverhampton (unpublished informal works.)

Report on an internal research study with humanities students to assess how hyperlinks to support materials help students engage with issues raised in tutor feedback.

Bartholomew, S. and Walsh, N. (2008) Unpacking tutor feedback, workshop. University of Wolverhampton (unpublished informal works).

Report on research with humanities students on issues obstacles facing students in unpacking and interpreting tutor feedback on essays.

Bastable, W., Ewart, K. and Cozens, L. (2008) Embedding information skills training on student learning: making a difference, in A. Wheeler (ed.) *Learning and Teaching Projects 2005–2007: Enhancing the Student Experience*. Wolverhampton: Institute for Learning Enhancement.

Short report on a collaborative approach between library staff and subject tutors in the development of information retrieval skills for students.

Bastable, W. and Morris, P. (2008) Embedding information skills training on student learning: providing the models, in A. Wheeler (ed.) *Learning and Teaching Projects 2005–2007: Enhancing the Student Experience*. Wolverhampton: Institute for Learning Enhancement.

Short report on a collaborative approach between library staff and subject tutors in the development of information retrieval skills for students.

Baynham, M. (2000) Academic writing in new and emergent discipline areas, in M. Lea and B. Stierer (eds) *Student Writing in Higher Education: New Contexts*. Buckingham: SRHE and Open University Press.

Chapter examines writing in disciplinary contexts in order to better understand problems confronted by novice writers.

Bazerman, C. (1989) Reading student texts: Proteus grabbing Proteus, in B. Lawson, S. Ryan and W.R. Winterowd (eds) *Encountering Student Texts: Interpretive Issues in Reading Student Writing*. Urbana, IL: NCTE.

Chapter discusses how ways that tutors read student texts impact on how students will write their assignments.

Beason, L. (1993) Feedback and revision in Writing Across the Curriculum classes. *Research in the Teaching of English*, 72(4): 395–422.

Takes a functionalist approach to academic literacies. Considers writing in a variety of genres as a way to promote understanding of purposes for writing in the disciplines.

Bellon, J.J., Bellon, E.C. and Blank, M.A. (1991) *Teaching from a Research Knowledge Base: A Development and Renewal Process.* Facsimile edition. Prentice Hall, New Jersey, USA.

Research found that when teachers effectively employ feedback procedures, they positively and often powerfully impact on the achievement of their students.

Berlin, J. (1988) Rhetoric and ideology in the writing class. *College English*, 50(5): 477–94.

Article examines university writing between 1928 and 1942.

Bevan, R., Badge, J., Cann, A., Willmott, C. and Scott, J. (2008) Seeing eye-to-eye? Staff and student views on feedback. *Bioscience Education*, 12(1). <http://www.bioscience.heacademy.ac.uk/journal/vol12/beej-12-1.aspx> (accessed 4 August 2009).

Useful article based on a survey with first year bioscience students on provision and utilization of feedback. Useful charts to show student views and also backed up by qualitative information from focus groups with students.

Biggs, J. (1999) *Teaching for Quality Learning at University*. Buckingham: Society for Research in Higher Education and Open University Press.

Highly important and usable book that provides practical advice for ways to improve teaching and learning in context of higher education. Considered a 'must read' by many educational theorists.

Biggs, J. (2003) *Teaching for Quality Learning at University*, 2nd edn. Buckingham: Open University Press.

An excellent resource for understanding and implementing an outcomes-based teaching and learning approach, which is helping students engage in a deep learning approach.

Black, P. and Wiliam, D. (1998a) Inside the black box: raising standards through classroom assessment. *Phi Delta Kappan*, 80(2): 139–49.

Influential pamphlet providing an extensive review of research literature that provides evidence to support their argument for the use of formative assessment, which both improves performance standards and increases learning gains.

Black, P. and Wiliam, D. (1998b) Assessment and classroom learning. *Assessment in Education*, 5(1): 7–74.

This article is a review of the literature on classroom formative assessment, showing firm evidence that innovations designed to strengthen the frequent feedback that students receive about their learning yielded improved performance.

Bloxham, S. and West, A. (2007) Learning to write in higher education: students' perceptions of an intervention in developing understanding of assessment criteria. *Teaching in Higher Education*, 12(1): 77–89.

Useful article that shares the results of a follow-up survey with students to see how they continue to apply input on feedback in later learning.

Bodner, G. M. (1986) Constructivism: a theory of knowledge. *Journal of Chemical Education*, 63: 873–8.

Provides an overview of paradigm shifts about ways of understanding knowledge and knowledge transfer, especially as related to the teaching of chemical engineering.

Boud, D. (2000) Sustainable assessment: rethinking assessment for the learning society. *Studies in Continuing Education*, 22(2): 151–67.

Interesting article that champions aligning assessment practices with long-term learning.

Boud, D. and Falchikov, N. (1989) Quantitative studies of student self-assessment in higher education: a critical analysis of findings. *Higher Education*, 18: 529–49.

Provides a critical review of the literature on self-assessment studies and argues that it is an essential part of the learning process that promotes work skills, lifelong learning and autonomy.

Boud, D. and Falchikov, N. (eds) (2007) *Rethinking Assessment in Higher Education: Learning for the Longer Term*. Abingdon: Routledge.

Very useful collection of articles, including the later entries for Ecclestone and Hounsell. Useful chapter by Boud and Falchikov on 'Assessment and emotion' which explores what it is like to be assessed.

Brannon, L. and Knoblauch, C.H. (1982) On students' rights to their own texts: a model of teacher response. *College Composition and Communication*, 33(2): 157–66.

Explores issues of control in student writing, and the role of tutors in assisting student development.

Brewer, R. (1996) *Exemplars: A Teacher's Solution*. Underhill, VT: Exemplars.

Offers advice about connecting students to topics and standards through the use of exemplars and rubrics.

Brooker, R., Muller, R., Mylonas, A. and Hansford, B. (1998) Improving the assessment of practice teaching: a criteria and standards framework. *Assessment & Evaluation in Higher Education*, 23(1): 5–20.

This paper reports on a two-stage development process of a criteria and standards framework for assessing final year practice teaching.

Brookhart, S.M. (2008) *How to Give Effective Feedback to Your Students.* Alexandria, VA: ASCD.

Slim little book that covers numerous aspects of giving feedback to school students, from what kinds of feedback work best to when and how often to give feedback.

Brown, S. and Glover, C. (2006) Evaluating written feedback, in C. Bryan and K. Clegg (eds) *Innovative Assessment in Higher Education.* London: Routledge.

A useful article which sets out research with Open University students to identity the aspects and types of feedback that students identify as useful.

Bruffee, K. (1986) Social construction, language, and the authority of knowledge: a bibliographical essay. *College English,* 48: 773–90.

Article that brings together voices from various disciplines that form a background for an argument that knowledge is social more than it is individual.

Bruner, J. (1970) Some theorems on instruction, in E. Stones (ed.) *Readings in Educational Psychology.* London: Methuen.

Influential input on understandings of learning.

Burke, D. (2007a) Engaging students in personal development planning: profiles, skills development and acting on feedback. *Discourse: Learning and Teaching in Philosophical and Religious Studies,* 6(2): 107–42.

Report on personal development planning approach with Religious Studies students, which focused on the benefits of resubmitting assignments in the light of tutor feedback.

Burke, D. (2007b) Getting the most out of feedback, in D. Nutt and J. Tidd (eds) *European First Year Experience: Conference April 2006,* Teesside, University of Teesside: 36–49.

An exploration of the benefits for student learning from tutor feedback by way of the Using Feedback Effectively form.

Burke, D. (2008) Using electronic sources to help students get more out of tutor feedback, in J. Pieterick, M. Lawton and R. Ralph (eds) *European First Year Experience Conference 2008,* University of Wolverhampton.

Report on the use of hyperlinks in tutor feedback to direct students to materials to enable students to follow up issues in feedback.

Burke, D. (2009a) Strategies for using feedback that students bring to their degree course: an analysis of first year perceptions at the start of a course in Humanities. *Assessment and Evaluation in Higher Education,* 34(1): 41–50.

Report on induction research with a large cohort of humanities students, which identified the range of starting points in relation to understandings of tutor feedback and its place in student learning.

Burke, D. (2009b) *Linked Learning: Hyperlinks in Feedback Webfolio.* http://pebblepad. wlv.ac.uk/webfolio.aspx?webfolioid=1112466 (accessed 30 June 2009).

Resource to support conference presentation at the Higher Education Academy conference in July 2009. Provides examples of resources used to support student learning from tutor feedback.

Burke, K. (1967) *Philosophy of Literary Form: Studies in Symbolic Action.* Baton Rouge: Louisiana State University Press.

Offers Burke's introduction to his important rhetorical theory of dramatism and provides a broad, useful approach for understanding various girders that theorists have constructed of how people use language within social contexts.

Butler, D.L. and Winne, P.H. (1995) Feedback and self-regulated learning: a theoretical synthesis. *Review of Educational Research,* 65(3): 245–81.

Article proposes five functions for feedback, which relate to academic content of essays.

Butler, R. (1987) Task-involving and ego-involving properties of evaluation: effects of different feedback conditions on motivational perceptions, interest, and performance. *Journal of Educational Psychology,* 79(4): 474–82.

Extensive study which identifies three feedback conditions: task involving (comments), ego involving (grades and praise), or neither (no feedback).

Cannon, D. (2002) Learning to fail: learning to recover, in M. Peelo and T. Wareham (eds) *Failing Students in Higher Education.* Buckingham: SRHE and Open University Press.

Chapter focuses on positive ways to help students cope with failing assignments.

Carino, P. (1991) Theorizing the writing center: an uneasy task, in R. Barnett and J. Blummer (eds) *The Allyn and Bacon Guide to Writing Center Theory and Practice.* Boston: Allyn and Bacon.

Chapter examines how social constructionism has influenced writing center theory.

Carless, D. (2006) Differing perceptions in the feedback process. *Studies in Higher Education,* 31(2): 219–33.

Research to explore tutor and student perceptions of the detail provided in feedback and student use of feedback for learning.

Carless, D. (2007) *How Assessment Supports Learning.* Hong Kong: Hong Kong University Press.

Exploration of key works on feedback, applied in the context of Hong Kong.

Catchpole, R. and Acres, D. (1995) Enhancing lecturer involvement in their students' learning skills development, in G. Gibbs (ed.) *Improving Student Learning: Through Assessment and Evaluation*. Oxford: The Oxford Centre for Staff Development.

Explores 'Action Booklets' as a way of enhancing lecturer involvement in supporting learners through feedback.

Chanock, K. (2000) Comments on essays: do students understand what tutors write? *Teaching in Higher Education*, 5(1): 95–105.

Study with history and politics students on their understandings of tutor feedback on their work.

Chinn, C.A. and Brewer, W.F. (1993) The role of anomalous data in science, religion, and magic, in K.S. Rosengren, C.N. Johnson and P.L. Harris (eds) *Imaging the Impossible: Magical, Scientific, and Religious Thinking in Children*. Cambridge: Cambridge University Press.

Chapter explores and recommends two strategies for engaging and increasing students' deep processing of information. Useful for understanding how peer interactions may encourage deep mental processing.

Chryssides, G.D. and Greaves, R. (2007) *The Study of Religion: An Introduction to Key Ideas and Methods*. London: Continuum.

Key work which sets study skills within a subject context.

CILIP (Chartered Institute of Library and Information Professionals) (2004) Information Literacy: definition. http://www.cilip.org.uk/professionalguidance/informationliteracy/definition/ (accessed 12 April 2004).

Key source for library and information staff that provides a definition and discussion of the term 'information literacy'.

Clouder, L. (1998) Getting the 'Right Answers': student evaluation as a reflection of intellectual development? *Teaching in Higher Education*, 3(2): 185–95.

Article highlights ways students' evaluative capabilities are dependent on their own beliefs and assumptions about 'ways of knowing'. Focuses primarily on student evaluations of teaching.

Coleman, I. (2001) Peer marking of formative assessments, in I. Moore (ed.) *Learning and Teaching Projects 2000–2001*. Wolverhampton: Centre for Learning and Teaching.

Short report on research with an introductory biomedical science module which involved students in marking formative assignments to help develop their understanding of the assessment process.

Connors, R.J. and Lunsford, A. (1993) Teachers' rhetorical comments on student papers. *College Composition and Communication*, 44: 200–24.

Studies writing teachers' rhetorical comments on student papers, including its historical background and as a recent phenomenon. Outlines basic patterns and types of teacher comments.

Cooper, N.J. (2000) Facilitating learning from formative feedback in Level 3 assessment. *Assessment and Evaluation in Higher Education*, 25(3): 279–91.

Article presents a strategy to change student approach to feedback, so they used feedback to reflect on their process of learning.

Corrywright, D. and Morgan, P. (2005) *Get Set for Religious Studies*. Edinburgh: Edinburgh University Press.

Series sets the development of study skills within the context of a discipline, Religious Studies, although some of the skills advice is generic and transferable.

Cottrell, S. (2001) *Teaching Study Skills and Supporting Learning*. Basingstoke: Palgrave.

This text accompanies texts for students on developing study skills. Provides some basic advice on student views on feedback.

Cramp, A. (2008) Developing student engagement with, and reflection on, feedback through the tutorial system, in A. Wheeler (ed.) *Learning and Teaching Projects 2005–2007: Enhancing the Student Experience*. Wolverhampton: Institute for Learning Enhancement.

Short article provides a summary of a project in the school of education to help students use tutor feedback systematically through tutorials.

Crisp, B.R. (2007) Is it worth the effort? How feedback influences students' subsequent submission of assessable work. *Assessment & Evaluation in Higher Education*, 32(5): 571–81.

Research highlights problems associated with providing effective feedback, particularly timing of feedback, and raises questions about why students may not take on feedback.

Daiker, D.A. (1989) Learning to praise, in C.M. Anson (ed.) *Writing and Response: Theory, Practice, and Research*. Urbana, IL: NCTE.

Chapter discusses the importance of positively responding to students' writing because students feel frustrated and come to hate writing when they see that most of the commentary on their papers is negative.

Davies, J. and Wrighton, N. (2004) Improving the attention students pay to, and the extent to which they act upon feedback, in H. Gale (ed.) *Learning and Teaching Projects 2003/2004*. Wolverhampton: Centre for Learning and Teaching.

Report on research within computing and information technology to improve the efficacy of the feedback process.

De Beaugrande, R. (1979) Psychology and composition. *College Composition and Communication*, 30: 50–7.

Early research on the psychology of language that sheds light upon crucial issues in the theory of composition.

Deci, E.L. (1972) Intrinsic motivation, extrinsic reinforcement, and inequity. *Journal of Personality and Social Psychology*, 22: 113–20.

Article is important for understanding student use of feedback in relation to attribution theory's 'discounting principle', in which decreased interest occurs because the subject discounts the role of intrinsic motivation when a salient extrinsic reward is present.

De Corte, E. (1996) New perspectives on learning and teaching in higher education, in A. Burgen (ed.) *Goals and Purposes of Higher Education in the 21st Century*. London: Jessica Kingsley.

Supports the standpoint that present understanding of productive learning as an active, constructive, collaborative and progressively more self-regulated process can guide the design of learning environments that have a high potential for boosting student competence.

Dempsey, J.V., Driscoll, M.P. and Swindell, L.K. (1993) Text-based feedback, in J.V. Dempsey and G.C. Sales (eds) *Interactive Instruction and Feedback*. Englewood Cliffs, NJ: Educational Technology Publications.

Influential chapter that looks at feedback used to promote learning within a cognitivist paradigm, concentrating on ways advanced technologies such as computers can deliver effective and useful feedback.

Devlin, M. (2002) Taking responsibility for learning isn't everything: a case for developing tertiary students' conceptions of learning. *Teaching in Higher Education*, 7(3): 125–38.

This study examines first year university student perceptions of responsibility for their learning, within the context of their conceptions of learning, with a view to meeting the objectives of higher education.

Dheram, P.K. (1995) Feedback as a two-bullock cart: a case study of teaching writing. *ELT Journal*, 49(2): 160–8.

Article argues that feedback is central to the process of learning and teaching and therefore both teachers and learners need to adopt a collaborative approach to monitoring and processing it. Tutors should assume the role of a facilitative consultant when providing feedback.

Dixon, H. and Williams, R. (2001) Teachers' understandings of formative assessment. Paper presented at the Annual Conference of the British Educational Research Association, University of Exeter. http://www.leeds.ac.uk/educol/documents/00002533.htm (accessed 11 August 2008).

Paper showed that while teachers accept basic idea that assessment has a positive role to play in the promotion of student learning, many do not know important differences between formative and summative assessments.

Dragga, S. (1992) *Technical Writing: Student Samples and Teacher Responses.* St. Paul, MN: Association of Teachers of Technical Writing.

Book provides samples of tutor responses to student texts and identifies commenting practices worth adopting/adapting when providing feedback to students' technical writing. Also examines use of collaborative writing and peer review.

Duffy, T.M. and Jonassen, D.J. (eds) (1992) *Constructivism and the Technology of Instruction: A Conversation.* Hillsdale, NJ: Lawrence Erlbaum.

Advocates a shift away from instructionist models of learning by creating constructivist learning environments that are supported by technology.

Duncan, N. (2007) 'Feed-forward': improving students' use of tutors' comments, *Assessment and Evaluation in Higher Education,* 32(3): 271–83.

Research in School of Education on student perceptions of tutor feedback and their view of the value of interventions in the process of writing an essay.

Duncan, N., Prowse, S., Burke, D. and Hughes, J. (2007) '. . . do that and I'll raise your grade.' Innovative module design and recursive feedback. *Teaching in Higher Education,* 12(4): 437–45.

Research in School of Education on student engagement with the opportunity to act on feedback on a draft before final submission.

Duncan, N., Prowse, S., Wakeman, C. and Harrison, R. (2004) Feed-forward; improving students' use of tutors' comments, in H. Gale (ed.) *Learning and Teaching Projects 2003–4.* Wolverhampton: Centre for Learning and Teaching.

Report on research in special needs and inclusion which used student assessment histories as a way of helping students see the relevance of feedback on one assignment to work in other areas.

Dunlap, J.C. (2005) Workload reduction in online courses: getting some shuteye. *Performance and Improvement,* 44(5): 18–25.

Considers the ways in which online peer review and collaboration can both enhance self-regulated learning and reduce tutor workload.

Dunlap, J.C. and Grabinger, S. (2003) Preparing students for lifelong learning: a review of instructional methodologies. *Performance Improvement Quarterly,* 16(2): 6–25.

Article examines the types of independent, self-directed learning and identifies benefits of students being able to engage in peer learning as it encourages reflection and leads to increased learning.

Dweck, C.S. (1999) *Self-theories: Their Role in Motivation, Personality, and Development.* Philadelphia, PA: The Psychology Press.

Intelligent and insightful book that summarizes and synthesizes 30 years of research on belief systems and their relationship to motivation and achievement.

Ecclestone, K. (1998) 'Just tell me what to do': barriers to assessment-in-learning in higher education. Scottish Educational Research Association Annual Conference, University of Dundee, 24–6 September.

Presents research to support the linking of formative and summative tasks in the design of assessment.

Ecclestone, K. (2007) Learning assessment, students' experiences in post-school qualifications, in D. Boud and N. Falchikov (eds) *Rethinking Assessment in Higher Education, Learning for the Longer Term.* Abingdon: Routledge.

Presents research from 2002 and Torrance et al. (2005) to consider challenges for students entering higher education.

Ede, L. (1989) On writing reading and reading writing, in B. Lawson, S. Ryan and W.R. Winterowd (eds) *Encountering Student Texts: Interpretive Issues in Reading Student Writing.* Urbana, IL: NCTE.

Chapter examines complexity of reading student writing and concludes that reading student essays becomes tantamount to writing them.

Elander, J., Harrington, K., Norton, L., Robinson, H. and Reddy, P. (2006) Complex skills and academic writing: a review of evidence about the types of learning required to meet core assessment criteria. *Assessment and Evaluation in Higher Education*, 31(1): 71–90.

Research analysed published assessment criteria in psychology, business studies and geography and found that critical thinking, use of language, structuring and argument were core criteria that have a central role in the shared perception of what is important in good student writing.

Elawar, M.C. and Corno, L. (1985) A factorial experiment in teachers' written feedback on student homework: changing teacher behaviour a little rather than a lot. *Journal of Educational Psychology*, 77(2): 162–73.

Article based on doctoral dissertation that advises the use of specific feedback that focuses equally on positive aspects of the work and inappropriate strategies or errors.

Elbow, P. (1973) *Writing Without Teachers.* New York: Oxford University Press.

One of the innovations in Elbow's method is the effort to distinguish between the skills and activities of creating and criticizing, getting writing done and then working on making the writing work for an audience.

Elbow, P. (1983) Embracing contraries in the teaching process. *College English* 45(4): 327–39.

Influential article that discusses the value of interdisciplinary teaching, Elbow's theory of 'cooking' (an interaction of conflicting ideas), the authority relationship in teaching and the value of specifying learning objectives. A full section is devoted to evaluation and feedback of both students and faculty.

Elbow, P. (1993) Ranking, evaluating, and liking: sorting out three forms of judgment. *College English*, 55(2): 187–206.

Highly inspirational article that attempts to distinguish different acts involved in assessment practices, and provides advice on different ways to express or frame value judgments when offering feedback to students on their writing.

Elbow, P. (1998) *Writing with Power: Techniques for Mastering the Writing Process*, 2nd Edn. Oxford: Oxford University Press.

A classic handbook that provides readers and writers with various methods for getting feedback; for getting words down on paper; for revising; for dealing with audience; and other 'recipes' for approaching writing.

Elliott, E.S. and Dweck, C.S. (1988) Goals: an approach to motivation and achievement. *Journal of Personality and Social Psychology*, 54(1): 5–12.

Article makes important connections between goal orientation and student motivation. Identifies difference between learning and performance goals and examines ways they can be central determinants of achievement patterns.

Emig, J. (1977) Writing as a mode of learning. *College Composition and Communication*, 28(2): 122–8.

Article considers the pros and cons of 'Writing across the curriculum' and 'Writing in the disciplines'. Its important contribution to feedback studies is the conclusion that writing, because it is both a process and product, serves as a 'unique' way of learning.

Faber, A. (1995) Praise that doesn't demean, criticism that doesn't wound. *American Educator*, 19(2): 33–8.

Describes constructive feedback that empowers students to do more and feel more positive about what they accomplish. Offers three examples of effective use of praise in feedback.

Faigley, L. (1986) Competing theories of process: a critique and a proposal. *College English*, 48(6): 527–42.

Seminal article that introduces a taxonomy for organizing contemporary composition theory.

Falchikov, N. (1995) Improving feedback to and from students, in P. Knight (ed.) *Assessment for Learning in Higher Education*. London: Kogan Page.

Article provides overview of the use of the term feedback, and sets out psychological issues affecting student perceptions of feedback.

Farr, J.L., Hoffman, D.A. and Ringenbach, K.L. (1993) Goal orientation and action control theory: implications for industrial and organizational psychology. *International Review of Industrial and Organizational Psychology*, 8: 193–232.

This study examined ways that goal orientation moderated the effects of feedback on effort, performance and self-efficacy over time.

Fedor, D.B., Davis, W.D., Maslyn, J.M. and Mathieson, K. (2001) Performance improvement efforts in response to negative feedback: the roles of source power and recipient self-esteem. *Journal of Management*, 27(1): 79–97.

Research investigated dimensions of authority and self-esteem as predictors of performance efforts following negative feedback.

Ferris, D. (1995) Student reactions to teacher response in multi-draft composition. *TESOL Quarterly*, 29: 33–53.

Examines ESL students' revision and editing in response to teacher commentary.

Ferris, D. (2003) *Response to Student Writing: Implications for Second Language Students*. Mahwah, NJ: Lawrence Erlbaum.

This book is aimed primarily at second language teachers, particularly those who teach writing classes, and reviews research into feedback given to second language writers. Also examines the practical issues of responding to student writing.

Ferris, D. and J.S. Hedgecock (1998) *Teaching ESL Composition: Purpose, Process, and Practice*. Mahwah, NJ: Lawrence Erlbaum.

Fairly comprehensive text that blends current reviews of ESL research with extensive coverage of practical topics related to the teaching of ESL writers in academic settings. Provides interesting insights about use of collaborative learning with second language users.

Fife, J.M. and O'Neill, P. (2001) Moving beyond the written comment: narrowing the gap between response practice and research. *College Composition and Communication*, 53(2): 300–21.

Article argues in favour of broadening notions of response and considering the varied ways students interpret and influence tutor feedback.

Flower, L. and Hayes, J.R. (1980) The dynamic of composing: making plans and juggling constraints, in L.W. Gregg and E.R. Steinberg (eds) *Cognitive Processes in Writing*. Hillsdale, NJ: Lawrence Erlbaum.

This work has probably had more impact on composition teaching practices than anything else in cognitive psychology, primarily because it shifted the focus of instruction away from the product and towards the writing process itself. Their model of the writing process is more of a 'task analysis' than a real model, however.

Flynn, E. and Schweickart, P. (1986) *Gender and Reading: Essays on Readers, Texts and Contexts*. Baltimore, MD: Johns Hopkins University Press.

Book brings together essays on feminist criticism, reading-research and reader-response criticism.

Gibbs, G. (2006) How assessment frames student learning, in C. Bryan and K. Clegg (eds) *Innovative Assessment in Higher Education*. London: Routledge.

Insight into research on feedback in The Open University from both staff and students.

Gibbs, G. and Simpson, C. (2004) *Does Your Assessment Support Your Students' Learning?* http://arts.unitec.ac.nz/documents/GrahamGibbAssessmentLearning.pdf (accessed 19 November 2009).

Article proposes 'conditions under which assessment supports learning' and includes a good review of research on feedback effectiveness.

Gitlin, A. and Smyth, J. (1989) *Teacher Evaluation: Educative Alternatives*. New York: Falmer Press.

Examines teacher evaluations, arguing they should be dialogical rather than hierarchical, and provides some interesting insights on creative dialogic feedback.

Goodrich Andrade, H. (1997) Understanding rubrics. *Educational Leadership*, 54(4): 14–17.

Argues that authentic assessments tend to use rubrics to describe student achievement.

Grant-Davie, K. and Shapiro, N. (1987) Curing the nervous tic: reader-based response to student writing. Paper presented at the Annual Meeting of the Conference on College Composition and Communication, March. http://www.eric.ed.gov/ERICWebPortal/custom/portlets/recordDetails/detailmini.jsp?_nfpb=true&_&ERICExtSearch_ Search Value_Ø=ED282196&ERICExtSearch_SearchType_Ø=no&accno=ED282196 (accessed 21 March 2009).

Conference paper shows that tutor commentary can have limited effect on the quality of student writing and the authors therefore advocate helping students become better readers and revisers of their own texts. Includes a helpful outline for a peer editing and revision workshop.

Graves, D. (1983) *Writing: Teachers and Children at Work*. Exeter, NH: Heinemann Educational Books.

Important work on writing processes in which the author offers advice to teachers about managing the process of teaching children to use the tools of the writing trade. The first part of the book focuses on teacher activity while the second part emphasizes children's growth through the writing process.

Grice, H.P. (1967) Logic and conversation. William James Lectures, 1967. Reprinted in H.P. Grice (ed.) *Studies in the Way of Words* (1989) Cambridge. MA: Harvard University Press.

Seminal work by important language philosopher that introduces the cooperative principle: a set of norms expected in conversation.

Griffin, C.W. (1982) Theory of responding to student writing: the state of the art. *College Composition and Communication*, 33: 296–301.

Examines some of the research on reasons for teachers' diverse reactions to student writing. Also looks at research on student reactions to teacher responses to their writing.

Haines, C. (2004) *Assessing Students' Written Work: Marking Essays and Reports.* London: RoutledgeFalmer.

Useful book in the 'Key Guides for Effective Teaching in Higher Education' series; provides an insight into research into student views on feedback on their work.

Harlen, W. and James, M.J. (1997) Assessment and learning: differences and relationships between formative and summative assessment. *Assessment in Education* 4(3): 365–80.

Article makes distinctions between two types of assessment as well as considers opportunities for using classroom events to gather information about the students.

Hattie, J. (2001) Influences on student learning: it's what you do second that makes a difference. http://www.geoffpetty.com/downloads/WORD/Influencesonstudent 2C683.pdf (accessed 18 April 2010).

Insightful and informal inaugural lecture that examines the role of feedback in student learning and achievement and offers a model of learning and teaching built on 'dollops of feedback'.

Hattie, J. and Timperly, H. (2007) The power of feedback. *Review of Educational Research*, 77(1): 81–112.

Important and insightful overview of formative feedback with useful advice on incorporating it in the classroom.

Hembree, R. (1988) Correlates, causes, and treatment of test anxiety. *Review of Educational Research*, 58: 47–77.

Hembree's research shows that the worry component is a stronger factor in test anxiety than the emotionality component.

Higgins, R., Hartley, P. and Skelton, A. (2001) Getting the message across: the problem of communicating assessment feedback. *Teaching in Higher Education*, 6(2): 269–74.

Article explores feedback as a form of communication and provides both a theoretical rationale and practical advice for helping students learn the purpose of feedback.

Hodges, E. (1997) Negotiating the margins: some principles for responding to our students' writing, some strategies for helping students read our comments, in M.D. Sorcinelli and P. Elbow (eds) *Writing to Learn: Strategies for Assigning and Responding to Writing Across the Disciplines*. San Francisco, CA: Jossey-Bass.

Chapter argues that the margins of students' written work are the ideal site for teacher-student conversations about that writing, but most of these conversations misfire, largely for reasons that are avoidable.

Hounsell, D. (1997) Contrasting perceptions of essay-writing, in F. Marton (ed.) *The Experience of Learning*. Edinburgh: Scottish Academic Press.

Considers the difficulty and tensions of writing academic essays and different disciplinary approaches to writing them.

Hounsell, D. (2003) Student feedback, learning and development, in M. Slowey and D. Watson (eds) *Higher Education and the Lifecourse*. London: Open University Press.

Chapter considers why feedback on student written work is in decline and attributes this to things like semesterization, modularization, large class sizes and marking procedures.

Hounsell, D. (2007) Towards more sustainable feedback to students, in D. Boud and N. Falichov (eds) *Rethinking Assessment in Higher Education*. Abingdon: Routledge.

Critique on place of feedback in HE with a suggestion for improvement.

Hyatt, D.F. (2005) Yes, a very good point!; a critical genre analysis of a corpus of feedback commentaries on Master of Education assignments. *Teaching in Higher Education*, 10(3): 339–53.

An analysis of sixty commentaries on scripts which identified key categories and explored their characteristics.

Hyland, F. (1998) The impact of teacher written feedback on individual writers. *Journal of Second Language Writing*, 7(3): 255–86.

Study suggests that tutors are aware of individual students and ways they may respond to tutor feedback and therefore tutors can tailor feedback accordingly.

Hyland, F. (2000) ESL writers and feedback: giving more autonomy to students. *Language Teaching Research*, 4(1): 33–54.

Article suggests that in some circumstances teachers should encourage students to take more responsibility for their own writing by allowing them to make their own decisions about their use and sources of feedback.

Hyland, F. and Hyland, K. (2001) Sugaring the pill: praise and criticism in written feedback. *Journal of Second Language Writing*, 10(3): 185–212.

Considers feedback in terms of how it functions as praise, criticism and suggestions, and explores tutor motivations for using these. Also examines cases where students failed to understand their teachers' comments due to their indirectness.

Irons, A. (2008) *Enhancing Learning through Formative Assessment and Feedback*. Abingdon: Routledge.

Detailed study on the benefit of formative assessment for student learning. It includes a range of useful summaries of case studies across disciplines.

Ivanič, R., Clark, R. and Rimmershaw, R. (2000) What am I supposed to make of this? The messages conveyed to students by tutors' comments, in M.R. Lea and B. Stierer (eds) *Student Writing in Higher Education: New Contexts*. Buckingham: SRHE and Open University Press.

Chapter examines ways feedback implies messages about the function of academic writing and the values and beliefs underpinning the institution.

Juwah, C., Macfarlane-Dick, D., Matthew, B., Nicol, D., Ross, D. and Smith, B. (2004) *Enhancing Student Learning through Effective Formative Feedback*. York: The Higher Education Academy Generic Centre.

Provides very useful information about designing formative assessments and aligning feedback.

Knight, P. (ed.) (1995) *Assessment for Learning in Higher Education*. London: Kogan Page.

Key edited text which provides a range of articles on feedback (see entries for Falichov and Race).

Knoblauch, C.H. and Brannon, L. (1981) Teacher commentary on student writing: the state of the art, in R. Graves (ed.) *Rhetoric and Composition: A Sourcebook for Teachers and Writers*. Upper Montclair, NJ: Boynton/Cook.

Argues that grading can diminish students' commitment to communicate ideas they value as well as the incentive to write.

Knoblauch, C.H. and Brannon, L. (1983) Writing as learning through the curriculum. *College English*, 45: 465–74.

Claims that their review of cross-disciplinary writing shows that numerous programmes are based on an erroneous assumption that knowledge is stable and bounded, while they should be based on the notion that knowing is an activity that involves making meaning from experience.

Kirkwood, M. (2007) The contribution of sustainable assessment, in D. Boud and N. Falchikov (eds) *Rethinking Assessment in Higher Education: Learning for the Longer Term*. Abingdon: Routledge.

Contends that feedback given in relation to the assessment criteria has value because it requires students to develop, apply and critique knowledge in context.

Kulhavy, R.W. and Stock, W.A. (1989) Feedback in written instruction: the place of response certitude. *Educational Psychology Review*, 1: 279–308.

Paper reviews written feedback from an information-processing perspective.

Kulhavy, R.W. and Wager, W. (1993) Feedback in programmed instruction: historical context and implications for practice, in J.V. Dempsey and G.C. Sales (eds) *Interactive Instruction and Feedback*. New Jersey: Educational Technology Publications.

Examines effects of feedback in context of programmed instruction.

Kvale, S. (2007) Contradictions of assessment for learning in institutions of higher learning, in D. Boud and N. Falichov (eds) *Rethinking Assessment in Higher Education: Learning for the Longer Term*. Abingdon: Routledge.

Considers psychological issues in learning and compares vocational and summative factors for the efficiency of feedback for learners.

Laurillard, D. (2002) *Rethinking University Teaching: A Conversational Framework for the Effective Use of Learning Technologies*, 2nd edn. London: Routledge.

Provides a sound theoretical basis for designing and using learning technologies in university teaching and considers usefulness of technologies of providing students with feedback.

Lave, J. and Wenger, E. (1991) *Situated Learning: Legitimate Peripheral Participation*. Cambridge: Cambridge University Press.

Attempts to move thinking away from theories of 'receiving' knowledge in favour of a focus on how real-world activities afford people access to knowledge that is fundamentally different from being spoon-fed or simply observing.

Lawson, B., Ryan, S. and Winterowd, W.R. (eds) (1989) *Encountering Student Texts: Interpretive Issues in Reading Student Writing*. Urbana, IL: NCTE.

Numerous chapters relevant to understanding the hermeneutical nature of reading and responding to student writing.

Lea, M.R. (2004) Academic literacies: a pedagogy for course design. *Studies in Higher Education*, 29(6): 739–56.

This article examines how research findings from the field of academic literacies might be used to underpin course design across the broad curriculum of higher education.

Lea, M.R. and Street, B. (1998) Student writing in higher education: an academic literacies approach. *Studies in Higher Education*, 23(2): 157–72.

Important work that introduces academic literacies approach to thinking about and teaching writing rather than as a skill.

Lea, M.R. and Street, B.V. (2000) *Student Writing and Staff Feedback in Higher Education: An Academic Literacies Approach*. Buckingham: SRHE and Open University.

Lea and Street's academic literacies approach stresses the need for students, faculty, and others to acknowledge the fundamentally underdetermined forms and conventions of academic writing and to work together for greater transparency in giving and getting feedback.

Leki, I. (1990) Coaching from the margins: issues in written response, in B. Kroll (ed.) *Second Language Writing: Research Insights for the Classroom*. New York: Cambridge University Press.

Chapter considers function of feedback for improving writing, and points out that many students prefer error correction methods that label mistakes and let them make corrections on their own.

Leki, I. (1991) The preferences of ESL students for error correction in college-level writing classes. *Foreign Language Annals*, 24(3): 203–18.

Presents the results of a survey of 100 ESL students in freshman composition classes and argues that teachers and students must agree about what constitutes improvement in writing. Suggests that students' expectations may need to be modified if students are to profit from teacher feedback.

Lewin, K. (1948) *Resolving Social Conflicts: Selected Papers on Group Dynamics* (ed. Gertrude W. Lewin). New York: Harper & Row.

Influential paper which argues that group dynamics and behaviours need to include a consideration of both the organization's structure and its environment.

Lillis, T. (2001) *Student Writing: Access, Regulation, Desire*. London: Routledge.

Important and thoughtful book that challenges ways of thinking about writing as a 'skill' and kick-starts the academic literacies approach.

Lillis, T. and Turner, J. (2001) Student writing in higher education: contemporary confusion, traditional concerns. *Teaching in Higher Education*, 6(1): 57–68.

Explores problems that exclude students from academic participation.

Lizzio, A. and Wilson, K. (2004) First-year students' perceptions of capability. *Studies in Higher Education*, 29(1): 109–28.

Study evaluated student self-perceptions of their level of capability across several domains of generic skills and attributes. Concluded that students' perceptions of the relevance of skills to their future work was the strongest predictor of their motivation for further learning.

Lunsford, R.F. (1997) When less is more: principles for responding in the disciplines, in M.D. Sorcinelli and P. Elbow (eds) *Writing to Learn: Strategies for Assigning and Responding to Writing Across the Disciplines*. San Francisco, CA: Jossey-Bass.

Offers basic guidelines for responding to student writing, and contends that teachers' comments should reflect their instructional goals for individual students.

MacLellan, E. (2001) Assessment for learning: the differing perceptions of tutors and students, *Assessment and Evaluation in Higher Education*, 26(4): 307–18.

Interesting information from study which reveals a gap between tutor and student perceptions of feedback.

Man, M. (2008) *The Etymology of Feedback*. http://www.manager-tools.com/2008/03/ the-etymology-of-feedback (accessed 22 May 2010).

Internet discussion group on feedback generally.

Marzano, R., Pickering, J. and McTighe, J. (1993) *Assessing Student Outcomes: Performance Assessment Using the Dimensions of Learning Model*. Alexandria, VA: ASCD.

Second part of the book provides examples of performance tasks and rubrics. Summary rubrics and rubrics for students to apply to tasks are also included.

Marzano, R., Pickering, J. and Pollock, D. (2001) *Classroom Instruction That Works: Research-based Strategies for Increasing Student Achievement*. Alexandria, VA: ASCD.

Draws on more than one hundred studies of classroom management to explain four important general components of effective classroom management and their impact on student engagement and achievement. Includes chapter on feedback and setting objectives.

McDowell, L. and Mowl, G. (1996) Innovative assessment: its impact on students, in G. Gibbs (ed.) *Improving Student Learning Through Assessment and Evaluation*. Oxford: The Oxford Centre for Staff Development.

Argues that peer assessment is one form of innovative assessment and has potential to improve the quality of learning and empower students.

McGinty, S. (2009) First year student voices: their experience of written feedback in a study skills module. Unpublished PhD thesis, University of Wolverhampton.

Research with first year students to explore their perceptions of the assessment process, particularly their views on aspects of tutor feedback that were helpful.

McKeachie, W.J. (1974) Instructional psychology. *Annual Review of Psychology*, 25: 161–93.

This review of the field of instructional psychology brought together studies on the factors that influence the effectiveness of instruction: the learner, the teacher, and the instructional process.

McLaughlin, P. (2008) *A System to Deliver Oral and Visual Feedback On-line, Personal to Each Student*. Centre for Bioscience, Higher Education Academy, York. http://www.bioscience.heacademy.ac.uk/ftp/DTES/mclaughlinwebrep.pdf (accessed 20 November 2009).

Research shows that using screen recording with an audio track to provide feedback on assignments allowed tutors to provide personalized and substantive feedback.

McMillan, K. and Weyers, J. (2005) *The Smarter Student*. Harlow: Pearson.

Text for students to explore skills and strategies for higher education. Contains a useful chart on areas for feedback and helps students unpack tutor comments.

McMillan, K. and Weyers, J. (2009) *The Smarter Study Skills Companion*. Harlow: Pearson.

Updated and expanded text to support student learning.

Mertler, C.A. (2001) Designing scoring rubrics for your classroom. *Practical Assessment, Research & Evaluation*, 7(25). http://PAREonline.net/getvn.asp?v=7&n=25 (accessed 19 November 2009).

Offers useful advice about designing and aligning rubrics for assessment.

Miller, S. (1982) How writers evaluate their own writing. *College Composition and Communication*, 33(2): 176–83.

Examines the modes of self-evaluation of writing quality and suggests that while writer resistance to self-evaluation may be healthy, without such evaluation, writers gain little from having written.

Moore, S., Neville, C., Murphy, M. and Connolly, C. (2010) *Ultimate Study Skills Handbook*. London: McGraw-Hill, Open University.

Text for students to encourage a reflective approach to learning. Chapters cover the range of skills that students need to develop in higher education. Particularly relevant for 'feedback' is the chapter 'Talking to the experts', with useful guidance for students to get the most out of their tutors.

Moreno, R. (2004) Decreasing cognitive load for novice students: effects of explanatory versus corrective feedback in discovery-based multimedia. *Instructional Science*, 32: 99–113.

Argues that feedback must be specific and clear or it will both impede learning and frustrate students.

Mory, E. (1992) The use of informational feedback in instruction: implications for future research. *Educational Technology Research and Development*, 40(3): 5–20.

Provides an overview of early research on feedback and advocates a shift from behavioural to information-processing perspective.

Murray, D. (1968) *A Writer Teaches Writing: A Practical Method of Teaching Composition*. Boston, MA: Houghton Mifflin.

Introduces the powerful idea that is central to all Murray's work, which is that we need to understand how writers write in order to teach writing effectively.

Murray, R. (2005) *Writing for Academic Journals*. Maidenhead: Open University Press.

Text for lecturers which explores issues about writing, writing blocks and offers practical solutions to challenges.

Murray, R. and Moore, S. (2006) *The Handbook of Academic Writing: A Fresh Approach*. Maidenhead: Open University Press.

Text designed for tutors which covers a wide range of aspects of academic writing, dealing with psychological, professional and practical aspects of writing.

Nicol, D. (1997) *Research on Learning and Higher Education Teaching*, UCoSDA Briefing Paper 45. Sheffield: Universities and Colleges Staff Development Agency.

Frequently cited briefing paper that examines strategies for self-regulated learning.

Nicol, D. (2007) Laying a foundation for lifelong learning: case studies of e-assessment in large 1st year classes. *British Journal of Educational Technology*, 38(4): 668–78.

Insightful article that argues for rethinking the purposes of feedback and formative assessment which more closely link to the development of learner self-regulation.

Nicol, D.J. and Macfarlane-Dick, D. (2006a) Formative assessment and self-regulated learning: a model and seven principles of good feedback practice. *Studies in Higher Education*, 31(2): 199–218.

This work re-interprets research on formative assessment and feedback, showing how these processes can help students take control of their own learning.

Nicol, D.J. and Macfarlane-Dick, D. (2006b) Rethinking Formative Assessment in HE: A Theoretical Model and Seven Principles of Good Feedback Practice. http://tltt.strath.ac.uk/REAP/public/Resources/DN_SHE_Final.pdf (accessed 18 May 2010).

Key paper considers how feedback can be used to help students develop self-regulated learning, and argue for the importance of both internal and external feedback in moving, or scaffolding, students towards learning in a more self-regulated way.

Nicol, D. and Milligan, C. (2006) Rethinking technology-supported assessment practices in relation to the seven principles of good feedback practice, in C. Bryan and K. Clegg (eds) *Innovative Assessment in Higher Education*. London: Routledge.

Explores self-regulated learning in the context of integrating online and face-to-face learning.

Northedge, A. (2003) Rethinking teaching in the context of diversity. *Teaching in Higher Education*, 8(1): 17–32.

Presents a response to challenges facing learners in higher education through a consideration of the socio-cultural approach to learning as learning subject discourses.

Norton, L.S. (1990) Essay writing: what really counts? *Higher Education*, 20(4): 411–42.

Findings, which are similar to Hounsell's, show that tutors and students often have quite different conceptions about the goals and criteria for essays in undergraduate courses.

NUS (National Union of Students) (2009) *HE Focus: The Great NUS Feedback Amnesty.* London: National Union of Students.

The first edition of the HE Focus journal focused on issues concerning feedback arising from the feedback amnesty.

Orrell, J. (2006) Feedback on learning achievement: rhetoric and reality. *Teaching in Higher Education,* 11(4): 441–56.

Useful article exploring benefits to students who took the option to take action on feedback.

Orsmond, P., Merry, S. and Reiling, K. (2000) The use of student derived marking criteria in peer and self-assessment. *Assessment and Evaluation in Higher Education,* 25(1): 23–37.

Exploration on contribution students can make to clarifying the purposes of assignments.

Orsmond, P., Merry, S. and Reiling, K. (2005) Biology students' utilisation of tutors' formative feedback: a qualitative interview study. *Assessment and Evaluation in Higher Education,* 30(4): 369–86.

Study reported that students see feedback as motivation 'to pursue their learning about a topic in a more independent fashion', and concluded that students received and utilized tutors' feedback in a variety of different ways connected to motivation, clarification, reflection and learning.

Paxton, M. (1998) Transforming assessment practices into learning processes, in S. Carter (ed.) *Access to Success: Literacy in Academic Contexts.* Lansdowne, SA: Juta Academic.

Explores the challenges facing students in learning how to write in the discipline of economics.

Penny, A.J. and Grover, C. (1996) An analysis of student grade expectations and marker consistency. *Assessment and Evaluation in Higher Education,* 21(2): 173–83.

Interesting research on the extent to which students misunderstand the criteria used to assess their final year research project.

Pieterick, J. (2009a) Margin(alised) comments: how students use feedback comments. University of Wolverhampton CIEL, Institute for Learning Enhancement, (unpublished staff development research seminar).

Paper uses small-scale classroom research to examine how students perceive and use placement of tutors' feedback comments to inform best practice.

Pieterick, J. (2009b) *CIEL Briefing Paper on Developing Academic Literacies.* University of Wolverhampton Institute for Learning Enhancement. www.wlv.ac.uk/default.aspx?page=18197 (accessed 23 November 2009).

Longitudinal study that uses quantitative tracking data and qualitative research to demonstrate the effectiveness of using cumulative coursework supported by e-tutoring to improve first year students' academic literacies and retention.

Podsakoff, P.M. and Farh, T. (1989) Effects of feedback sign and credibility on goal setting and task performance. *Organizational Behavior and Human Decision Processes*, 44(1): 45–67.

Laboratory-based study that looked at feedback credibility in relation to goal setting.

Porter, A. (2009) NUS – working to improve assessment feedback. *HE Focus: The Great NUS Feedback Amnesty*, 1(1): 1. London: National Union of Students.

Statement of ten principles for feedback from the perspective of the National Union of Students.

Price, M. and O'Donovan, B. (2006) Improving performance through enhancing student understanding of criteria and feedback, in C. Bryan and K. Clegg (eds) *Innovative Assessment in Higher Education*. London: Routledge.

Chapter reports on benefits identified from a workshop that helped students unpack tutor feedback on their work and compare it with their own self-assessment.

Prosser, M. and Webb, C. (1994) Relating the process of undergraduate essay writing to the finished product. *Studies in Higher Education*, 19(2): 125–38.

Article explores the challenges facing students in understanding the concept of an essay.

Purves, A.C. (1984) The teacher as reader: an anatomy. *College English*, 46(3): 259–65.

Article explores three issues related to the activity of writing and examines the issue of audience for student writing, creating a number of possibilities.

Quality Assurance Agency for Higher Education (2000) Section 6. Assessment of Students, from 'Code of practice for the assurance of academic quality and standards in higher education'. http://www.qaa.ac.uk/academicinfrastructure/codeOfPractice/default.asp (accessed 30 October 2006).

Official UK requirements for standards in higher education; this section sets out requirements for assessment and feedback.

Race, P. (1995) What has assessment done for us – and to us? In P. Knight (ed.) *Assessment for Learning in Higher Education*. London: Kogan Page.

Range of practical suggestions to develop assessment and feedback to help students benefit from tutor advice.

Race, P. (1997) Why assess innovatively? in S. Brown and A. Glasner (eds) *Assessment Matters in Higher Education*. Buckingham: SHRE and Open University Press.

Provides a theoretical rationale for incremental changes to assessment practices.

Race, P. (2001) *Using Feedback to Help Students to Learn*. York: Higher Education Academy.

Pamphlet provides a theoretical framework for the purpose of feedback in relation to student learning, and offers practical suggestions for implementation.

Race, P. (2005) *Making Learning Happen: A Guide for Post-compulsory Education*. London: Sage.

Intelligent, accessible and highly usable book on feedback and learning that centres on Professor Race's 'ripples in the pond' model.

Race, P. (2007) *How to Get a Good Degree*, 2nd edn. Maidenhead: Open University Press.

Second edition contains a new chapter 'Building on feedback', with activities to help students make more use of tutor feedback.

Race, P., Brown, S. and Smith, B. (2005) *500 Tips on Assessment*, 2nd edn. London: Routledge.

Very useful and accessible book containing practical advice and numerous practices worth adopting for assessment practices in higher education.

Radecki, P. and Swales, J. (1988) ESL student reaction to written comments on their written work. *System*, 16(3): 355–65.

Research on feedback to ESL students showed that the students preferred their instructors to edit grammatical and other mechanical errors because they believed such comments to be the most helpful.

Ramaprasad, A. (1983) On the definition of feedback. *Behavioural Science*, 28(1): 4–13.

Explains feedback from a management and industry perspective but has been widely adapted for educational discussions on formative feedback.

Rawson, M. (2000) Learning to learn: more than a skill set. *Studies in Higher Education*, 25(2): 226–38.

This article raises the question of whether learning to learn should be regarded purely as a skill

Reid, J. (1994) Responding to ESL students' texts: the myths of appropriation. *TESOL Quarterly*, 28(2): 273–92.

Interesting and provocative article that reviews the historical bases for the appropriation issue in first and second language writing classrooms. It encourages teachers to use their roles as writing experts and cultural informants to empower students in their writing.

Rennie, C. (2000) Error feedback in ESL writing classes: what do students really want? Unpublished master's thesis, California State University, Sacramento, CA.

Postgraduate research on feedback showed that both ESL students and teachers preferred direct, explicit feedback rather than indirect feedback.

Ridley, D. (2004) Puzzling experiences in higher education: critical moments for conversation. *Studies in Higher Education*, 29(1): 91–107.

The article emphasizes the social nature of learning and argues that tutors should respond flexibly to students' needs by providing varying degrees of explicit guidance and less conspicuous facilitation through interaction and participation.

Robinson, A. and Udall, M. (2006) Using formative assessment to improve student learning through critical reflection, in C. Bryan and K. Clegg (eds) *Innovative Assessment in Higher Education*. London: Routledge.

This chapter presents the goals and principles of a learning and teaching approach designed to help students make more realistic judgements about their own learning.

Rorty, R. (1989) *Contingency, Irony and Solidarity*. Cambridge: Cambridge University Press.

Work by influential analytical philosopher, which sets out his theory that meaning is a socio-linguistic construction.

Rust, C. (2002) The impact of assessment on student learning: how can research literature practically help to inform the development of departmental strategies and learner-centred assessment practices? *Active Learning in Higher Education*, 3(2): 145–58.

Useful survey of research findings on the impact of feedback on student learning.

Rust, C., O'Donovan, B. and Price, M.A. (2005) Social constructivist assessment process model: how the research literature shows us this could be best practice. *Assessment and Evaluation in Higher Education*, 30(3): 231–40.

Article argues in favour of using social constructivist approach to assessment as a way of enhancing student learning. Also provides helpful examples.

Rust, C., Price, M.A. and O'Donovan, B. (2003) Improving students' learning by developing their understanding of assessment criteria and processes. *Assessment and Evaluation in Higher Education*, 28(2): 147–64.

Article shows that student learning can be enhanced significantly when they have an understanding of assessment criteria and processes. Also discusses use of assessment rubrics.

Sadler, D.R. (1989) Formative assessment and the design of instructional systems. *Instructional Science*, 18: 119–44.

Offers a broader definition of feedback by including dialogues that support learning, which are fundamental to the process of 'closing the loop' in assessment.

Schreyer Institute for Teaching Excellence (2007) *The Basics of Rubrics*. Penn State University. http://www.schreyerinstitute.psu.edu/pdf/RubricBasics.pdf (accessed 19 November 2009).

Provides useful advice about designing assessment rubrics in tertiary education.

Schwartz, P. and Webb, G. (eds) (2002) *Assessment: Case Studies, Experience and Practice from Higher Education.* London: Kogan Page.

Covers numerous key topics in assessment, and includes interesting cases from the UK, the United States, Australia and New Zealand that cover traditional and contemporary assessment techniques.

Shute, V.J. (2008) Focus on formative feedback. *Review of Educational Research,* 78: 153–89.

A fairly comprehensive review of the expansive body of feedback research that deals primarily with formative feedback. Provides practical advice about using formative feedback based on scholarship.

Skinner, B.F. (1958) Reinforcement today. *American Psychologist,* 13: 94–9.

Seminal work on the temporal relationships between behaviour and reinforcement.

Smart, N. (1989) *The World's Religions: Old Religions and Modern Transformations.* Cambridge: Cambridge University Press.

Key text setting out Smart's dimensions in a historical overview of the major religions.

Smith, D., Campbell, J. and Brooker, R. (2001) The impact of students' approaches to essay writing on the quality of their essays. *Assessment and Evaluation in Higher Education,* 24(3): 327–38.

Shows that students' approaches to essay writing seem to be inter-related in complex and often reciprocal ways, and relate directly or indirectly to higher education learning outcomes.

Smith, S. (1997) The genre of the end comment: conventions in teacher responses to student writing. *College Composition and Communication,* 48(2): 249–68.

Research that examined over 200 end comments made on student texts.

Snyder B.R. (1971) *The Hidden Curriculum.* New York: Alfred A. Knopf.

Dated but still relevant book that contends two curriculums govern university degrees. In addition to mastering the substantive, disciplinary one, a student must cope with the 'playing the academic game' whereby appropriate responses to institutional prejudices ensure a high degree classification.

Sommers, N. (1982) Responding to student writing. *College Composition and Communication,* 33(2): 148–56.

Interesting perspective from the standpoint of a writing tutor, to consider impact of tutor intervention on student work.

Sommers, N. (2006) Across the drafts. *College Composition and Communication,* 58(2): 248–57.

Sommers revisits the work on tutor feedback she began in 'Responding to student writing' by following 400 Harvard undergraduates throughout their academic careers. She concludes that students need numerous opportunities to practise writing and advocates the need for a transactional experience that pairs honest critique and instruction.

Spandel, V. and Stiggins, R.J. (1990) *Creating Writers: Linking Assessment and Writing Instruction.* New York: Longman.

Suggest writing evaluation can be improved through use of large-scale assessment practices such as analytic and holistic scoring guides.

Sprinkle, R.S. (2004) Written commentary: a systematic, theory-based approach to response. *Teaching English in the Two-Year College,* 31(2): 273–86.

A consideration of different approaches to comments, and implications arising from tutor control over student revision.

Stephani, L.A. (1998) Assessment in partnership with learners. *Assessment and Evaluation in Higher Education,* 23(4): 339–50.

Article explores the importance of students understanding assessment criteria and advises tutors on how 'good feedback on learning' can help students make the link to assessment criteria.

Storch, N. and Tapper, J. (2000) The focus of teacher and student concerns in discipline-specific writing by university students. *Higher Education Research and Development,* 19(3): 337–55.

Interesting article on discipline-specific writing and student-tutor perceptions of assignment purpose, which shows a mismatch between tutor feedback and assignment purpose.

Straub, R. (1996) The concept of control in teacher response: defining the varieties of 'directive' and 'facilitative' commentary. *College Composition and Communication,* 47(2): 223–51.

Evaluates the different comments made by composition teachers in order to define a way to label and interpret comments and encourage tutors to re-examine and improve their written comments on student essays.

Straub, R. (1997) Students' reactions to teacher comments: an exploratory study. *Research in the Teaching of English,* 31: 91–119.

This article presents the results of a survey of 142 first-year university writing students' perceptions about teacher comments on a writing sample and uses students' responses to identify types of feedback commentary they found most useful.

Straub, R. (1999) *A Sourcebook for Responding to Student Writing.* Cresskill, NJ: Hampton Press.

A practical guide that examines ways of responding to student writing. Provides models of teacher comments and discussions about response as a way of developing personal response style.

Straub, R. (2000) *The Practice of Response: Strategies for Commenting on Student Writing*. Cresskill, NJ: Hampton Press.

Insightful book that attempts to demonstrate effective teacher response is a matter of putting into practice certain accepted principles of response.

Straub, R. (2002) Reading and responding to student writing: a heuristic for reflective practice. *Composition Studies*, 30(1): 15–60.

Useful article that constructs a protocol of a teacher reading and responding to a student essay.

Struyven, K., Dochy, F. and Janssens, S. (2005) Students' perceptions about evaluation and assessment in higher education: a review. *Assessment and Evaluation in Higher Education*, 30(4): 325–41.

Article examines evaluation and assessment from the student's point of view and explores student perceptions and behaviour in relation to assessment modes and methods.

Tait, H., Speth, C. and Entwistle, N. (1996) Identifying and advising students with deficient study skills and strategies, in G. Gibbs (ed.) *Improving Student Learning Through Assessment and Evaluation*. Oxford: The Oxford Centre for Staff Development.

Describes three main areas of activity in a project designed to develop a computer-based package to identify students in higher education, who are at risk due to ineffective study skills and strategies, and then to advise them.

Tang, R. (2000) Do we allow what we encourage? How students are positioned by teacher feedback. *The Australian Journal of Language and Literacy*, 23(2): 157–68.

Interesting and useful article that considers feedback in relation to power and identity. Identifies numerous roles tutors play in feedback situations and suggests they choose roles according to feedback purposes.

Taras, M. (2001) The use of tutor feedback and student self-assessment in summative assessment tasks: towards transparency for students and tutors. *Assessment and Evaluation in Higher Education*, 26(6): 605–14.

Article argues that re-submission is the best way to check if students have understood and internalized tutor feedback.

Taras, M. (2003) To feedback or not to feedback in student self-assessment. *Assessment and Evaluation in Higher Education*, 28(5): 549–65.

Presents research to show the value that tutor feedback makes to the process of student self-assessment.

Taras, M. (2006) Do unto others or not: equity in feedback for undergraduates. *Assessment and Evaluation in Higher Education*, 31(3): 365–77.

Article argues that undergraduate students should experience the same process as tutors in developing ideas, with the opportunity to act on feedback in a series of iterative cycles.

Tierney, R. and Simon, M. (2004) What's still wrong with rubrics: focusing on the consistency of performance criteria across scale levels. *Practical Assessment, Research & Evaluation*, 9(2). Retrieved from http://PAREonline.net/getvn.asp?v=9&n=2 (accessed 14 June 2009).

Examines performance criteria descriptors used in rubrics and provides advice about creating or adapting scoring rubrics.

Topping, K. (1998) Peer assessment between students in colleges and universities. *Review of Educational Research*, 68(3): 249–76.

Very interesting article that provides a typology of peer assessment and examines research in order to conclude that peer assessment is reliable and valid across a variety of applications.

Torrance, T., Colley, H., Garratt, D. et al. (2005) *The Impact of Different Modes of Assessment on Achievement and Progress in the Learning and Skills Sector*. http:www.Isda.org.uk/cims/order.aspx?code=052284&src=XOWEB (accessed 22 May 2010).

Research on challenges for students entering higher education.

Tunstall, P. and Gipps, C. (1996) Teacher feedback to young children in formative assessment: a typology. *British Educational Research Association*, 22(4): 389–404.

Article provides a topology of formative feedback and makes clear distinctions between descriptive and evaluative commentary.

Uemlianin, I.A. (2000) Engaging text: assessing paraphrase and understanding. *Studies in Higher Education*, 25(2): 347–58.

Article examines students' paraphrases to set text as demonstration of understanding kinds of information and considers its relevance for student feedback.

Walker, M. (2009) An investigation into written comments on assignments: do students find them usable? *Assessment & Evaluation in Higher Education*, 34(1): 67–78.

Recent and relevant research which provides student perceptions of feedback.

Weaver, M.R. (2006) Do students value feedback? Student perceptions of tutors' written response. *Assessment and Evaluation in Higher Education*, 31(3): 379–94.

Interesting study with wide range of charts presenting detailed information on views of business and design students.

Wicklow, K. (2009) Students, the experts in their own learning. *HE Focus: The Great NUS Feedback Amnesty*, 1(1): 1. London: National Union of Students.

National Student Union officer's perspective on the importance of feedback for student learning.

Wiggins, G. (1997) Feedback: how learning occurs. A presentation from the 1997 AAHE Conference on Assessment & Quality. Pennington, NJ: The Center on Learning, Assessment, and School Structure.

Argues that excellence is attained through the feedback that is cyclical and such cycles typically take the form of 'model-practice-perform-feedback-perform'.

Wiggins, G. (2004) Assessment as feedback. New Horizons for Learning. http://www.newhorizons.org (accessed 15 June 2009).

Considers differences between formative and summative feedback, and argues that feedback as guidance is more effective.

Williams, K. (2005) Lecturer and first year student (mis)understandings of assessment task verbs: 'Mind the gap'. *Teaching in Higher Education*, 10(2): 157–73.

Research examined chemistry students' interpretations of assessment task verbs and concluded that a significant gap existed between students' and tutors' understanding.

Williams, J. and Kane, D. (eds) (2008) *Exploring the National Student Survey: Assessment and Feedback Issues*. Executive summary. York: The Higher Education Academy.

The summary provides lists of examples of good practice in relation to assessment and feedback.

Winter, C. and Dye, V. (2004) An investigation into the reasons why students do not collect marked assignments and the accompanying feedback, in H. Gale (ed.) *Learning and Teaching Projects 2003/2004*. Wolverhampton: Institute for Learning Enhancement.

Short article within education studies to explore reasons why students do not collect assignments.

Wootton, S. (2002) Encouraging learning or measuring failure? *Teaching in Higher Education*, 7(3): 353–7.

Considers negative impact of assessment on 'at risk' students and asks whether the system intends to measure failure or encourage learning.

Yorke, M. (2000) The rear-view mirror tells a story: subject area differences in undergraduate non-completion and their implications for the improvement of learning in higher education, in C. Rust (ed.) *Improving Student Learning Through the Disciplines*. Oxford: Oxford Centre for Staff and Learning Development.

Research showed that the inability to keep up academically in subject disciplines was a major factor in explaining students' decisions to withdraw from university.

Yorke, M. (2001) Turn first-semester assessments into richer learning experiences. *Innovations in Education and Teaching International*, 38(3): 277–8.

Elaborates on the positive or negative ways in which formative assessment can affect student retention.

Yorke, M. (2002) Academic failure: a retrospective view from non-completing students, in M. Peelo and T. Wareham (eds) *Failing Students in Higher Education*. Maidenhead: SRHE and Open University Press.

Advocates the need for tutors to spend time helping students to use the feedback they receive.

Yorke, M. (2003) Formative assessment in higher education: moves towards theory and the enhancement of pedagogic practice. *Higher Education*, 45: 477–501.

Argues in favour of using formative assessments because the need to perform for high-stakes summative assessments at the end of the first semester frequently applies excessive pressure on those who are acclimatizing themselves to university.

Yorke, M. and Longden, B. (2008) *The First-year Experience of Higher Education in the UK (Final Report)*. York: Higher Education Academy.

Reports the findings of FYE survey, which indicates that the issues raised by students who fail to continue with their courses are very similar to those raised ten years ago.

Young, P. (2000) 'I might as well give up': self-esteem and mature students' feelings about feedback on assignments. *Journal of Further and Higher Education*, 24(3): 409–18.

Research that examined Access students' attitudes towards feedback that showed mature students' attitudes to receiving feedback and their perceptions of the messages they were receiving were highly varied.

Zamel, V. (1985) Responding to student writing. *TESOL Quarterly*, 19(1): 86–96.

Zamel's work on the effectiveness of teacher feedback on second language writing does not support a focus on surface error to help students improve their writing.

Zimmerman, B.J. and Schunk, D.H. (1989) *Self Regulated Learning and Academic Achievement: Theory, Research and Practice*. Hillsdale, NJ: Erlbaum.

Book pulls together research on different theoretical perspectives of students' self-regulation of learning.

Index

Related books from Open University Press

Purchase from www.openup.co.uk or order through your local bookseller

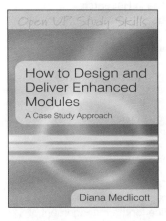

HOW TO DESIGN AND DELIVER ENHANCED MODULES

Diana Medlicott

9780335233977 (Paperback)
2009

eBook also available

- Would you like to make the modules you teach more engaging?
- Do you want to deliver enjoyable and effective learning?
- Are you interested in a model that has been proven to work?
- Would you like to evaluate the quality of what you deliver?

Key features:

- Includes sections on design, and delivery and evaluation
- It details practical ideas for seminars, lectures, assessment, feedback and student support
- Provides key reading for all those interested in improving student learning and retention

www.openup.co.uk

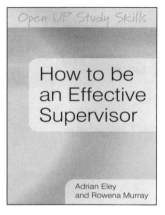

HOW TO BE AN EFFECTIVE SUPERVISOR
Best Practice in Research Student Supervision

Adrian Eley and Rowena Murray

9780335222957 (Paperback)
2009

eBook also available

This timely new book is based on the precepts of the Quality Assurance Agency's recent Code of Practice for the management of Postgraduate Research Programmes. It presents practical information on the QAA Code of Practice, to serve both as a ready reference source for supervisors and as a manual for research supervisor training.

Key features:

- Examples of problems and suggested solutions
- Guides supervisors through issues they may face
- Provides recommendations for further reading

www.openup.co.uk

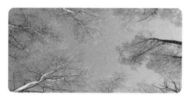